The Daily Journal of
Kindness

The
Daily Journal of
Kindness

A Guide for Creating
Your Own Kindness
Revolution

HANOCH AND MELADEE MCCARTY

Health Communications, Inc.
Deerfield Beach, Florida

©1996 Hanoch and Meladee McCarty
ISBN 1-55874-412-6

Publisher: Health Communications, Inc.
            3201 S.W. 15th Street
            Deerfield Beach, Florida 33442-8190

Cover design by Lawna Patterson Oldfield

To our nephew,
Adam Scott Bendell,
who travels ever so gently on
the path to enlightenment
and personal growth.
His presence in our lives
reminds us that it is possible to
walk softly and with great
humor through this life.
His love and playfulness
are the kindest
gift to us.
And also to Uncle Harry
Schultz, a model of kindness,
a mentor of spirituality,
and the giving conduit of
laughter and fun. Your spirit
is with us for all time.

The greatest challenge of the day is: how to bring about a revolution of the heart, a revolution which has to start with each one of us.

—Dorothy Day

Nobody has ever measured, not even poets, how much the heart can hold.

—Zelda Fitzgerald

Acknowledgments

∙∙

Special thanks to our children Shayna, Ethan, Mac and Stephanie who model kindness for us on a regular basis and who have often given us their fresh and vibrant perspective as they discover opportunities to express kindness in the world.

Our thanks also to Scottie Borges, whose loving kindness knows no limits and whose depth of spirit transcends age and size.

Our gratitude always to Sidney and Suzanne Simon for their support and many ideas, to Doug Bendell for his tender love, to Eric Spiess for showing that kindness lives in deeds as well as words, to A. Gringa Parnussa for proving that excitement is never "just a Schmenge," and to all the very kind people all over America who wrote to us to share kindness ideas and stories after reading our first book, *Acts of Kindness: How to Create a Kindness Revolution.*

Finally and very importantly, our deepest thanks to our eternally patient and maximally supportive editor, Christine Belleris. Her guidance and her gentle advice have always been of inestimable worth.

How to Use This Kindness Journal

....

*Th*is is not just another meditations/affirmations book. It is not simply another kind of calendar. We've designed it to be a journal in which you can work out the role that kindness can play in your life. It is a guided journey through your days, seeking to develop an increasingly rich and deepening conception of kindness and how it can bring meaning, value and joy into every moment.

The book is organized into the four seasons, winter, spring, summer and fall. Each month is represented, as is every day of the year. Because this book is meant to last for years and years, we've set a sort of "weekend retreat" of journal-writing opportunities every seven days. They do not necessarily fall on weekends, but may be treated as such.

You'll find what we hope will be an inspiring or thought-provoking quote on every day of the year. Only the weekend retreat days are structured with questions for thought and response, but space is provided on every day for your thoughts and your questions and, especially, your responses.

We urge you to *use* this book, *write in* this book, *talk* to this book. Because both of us have been teachers of children and of adults, we've learned that in the act of asking questions and of answering them, there is great opportunity for learning. Even questions to which we thought we knew the answers, when asked again—especially in a new context or in juxtaposition with a stimulating quote—we've learned more and relearned more than we knew that we knew! This book is created in that spirit. It is intended to help go beneath and beyond an obvious and simplistic conception of kindness and to finally help realize kindness through ownership of kind ideas and through application of kind thoughts to one's own life.

There are also special holiday pages filled to the brim with unusual ideas on how to express kindness for every major holiday during the year.

Holidays that always fall on the same day every year, such as New Year's Day and Valentine's Day, can be found in their proper place. We've placed holidays that vary from year to year at the beginning of the appropriate month so that you can plan ahead.

We hope that you will share these ideas with your friends, your neighbors, your family members and your co-workers. Our not-so-hidden agenda is to start a Kindness Revolution in America. We think it's time for civility, service, empathy, caring, tenderness, concern for others and self-responsibility to be returned to our country and to the world. You can be part of that by simply choosing to do one *deliberate act of kindness* every day.

The word, *journal*, comes from the French word, *jour*, which means *day*. A journey is the distance one can travel in a day and a journal is the record of one's "journey through the days." One of the essential elements of journaling, or of living more thoughtfully, is the act of keeping a daily journal. In that journal, you write your deepest thoughts and concerns, your daily experience of events and your experience of yourself in those events, and the meanings that your life seems to take on as these events ebb and flow.

We think that you'll get the most benefit from this

book by reading a page every day and pausing in the rush of your life to think about the idea on that page, specifically as to how it applies to your life. When you have a bit more time, we think you might want to try the nearest "weekend retreat." Go to those pages and think through, work through, and write through the questions and thoughts on that page.

We know that memory can fade. Insight comes and goes. You can get a startling insight on Monday and, because of the many things that occupy and distract us all, you may have totally forgotten it by Wednesday! Therefore we recommend that you consider writing your responses right here in the book. Also, this book will become a part of your own personal history. Rereading the pages with your comments and thoughts on them, years from now, will bring you a clear appreciation of the developmental process of your life and thought. Going through those same pages for a second year will undoubtedly strike new notes in your thinking, and you'll be able to find spaces to add second and third thoughts as you go on. This book can definitely be recycled in this way.

We think that most people will gain many ideas about kindness from this journaling process. People have told us that some of these pages have stimulated letters to family members, discussions, apologies, breakthroughs in "impacted" relationships. The magic, however, is not inherent in our ideas or in the particular way we've expressed them in this book. Instead it lies solely in your commitment to self-discovery and healing that keeping a journal about kindness implies.

We wish you the very best. As you attain an insight that is new or valuable to you, or as a memory of an experience of kindness comes up for you, feel free to write to us and share it with us. We love to hear from our readers and fellow journalers. We might even write to you asking permission to use your insight or your story in one of our next book projects. In any event, be sure that we really do care. And we want to do our part to help create a kinder world.

Twelve Steps to a Kinder Life

....

Deliberate Acts of Kindness with Life-Affirming Consequences

1. **Do It Now.** Be kind. Smile. Consider the other person's feelings. Don't wait till later. Now is the time to be kind. "Today is a gift, tomorrow is only a promise." Be kind now.

2. **Start Small.** Kindness doesn't have to be flamboyant, dramatic, time-consuming or expensive. The little kindnesses will do for now. "We must *be* the changes we want to create in the world."
   —Mahatma Ghandi.

3. **There Are No Prerequisites or Tests for Kindness.** It is very possible to be kind even though bad things are happening elsewhere. We each make the world just that much kinder and safer for others when we choose to be kind today. Don't wait for the world's big problems to be solved before you take kind action.

4. **Get in the Habit of Kindness.** When kindness is built into your life, it will not seem remarkable, nor will it be extra effort. It will just be the way you *are.* And everyone in your life will behave toward you based on that idea of who you are!

5. **Keep It Safe.** Safe for you and safe for the recipient. Make sure no one gets embarrassed or put-upon because of your desire to do a kindness.

6. **Don't Seek Gratitude.** Do kindness because it's the right thing, not because you'd like recognition. "The highest kindness is that which is done anonymously."   —Rabbi Moses Maimonides.

7. **Enjoy Your Own Kindness.** There's a joy and deep satisfaction in being kind and considerate of others. Let that feeling fill you, heal you, and help you find the energy and courage to go on.

8. **Look Around Your World for Kindness—You'll Find It.** Page through the paper looking for kindnesses and cut out the articles you find for just one week. You'll be surprised at how many there are. Look for the kindnesses that others are doing. Tell them you appreciate them. Become "fellow kindness revolutionaries." Let your friends, colleagues and family know about the good that you see; it will help them see it too.

9. **Don't Compare Yourself to Anyone Else.** Don't use a secret "kindness meter" to always judge yourself. If someone else does a great kindness, don't compete with it—instead you can join it, learn from it, copy it gratefully, extend it.

10. **Allow Yourself to Be a Receiver Of Kindness.** It's just not possible to be a giver all the time. It is an act of kindness to be the receiver of someone else's help. After all, they need someone to be kind to, don't they?

11. **Refraining Can Be a Great Act of Kindness:** refrain from yelling; refrain from jumping to conclusions or judging people harshly; refrain from put-downs, sarcasm, negative characterization of

others or gossip. Sometimes what you choose *not* to do is as important as what you choose *to* do!

12. **Do Your Job Today with Quiet Competence.** Whatever it is you do, just simply do it well, to your fullest ability, with all your creativity and artistry and whatever joy you can muster. Think of what a kindness it will be to everyone you deal with. Don't complain, evade, mutter, sulk or goof off. Do your job and do it well. Consider how frustrating it is to you when you enter a business and the employees seem resentful, lackadaisical, uncaring or distant. Or how disappointing it can be when a member of your family does a chore with obvious disdain or constant whining.

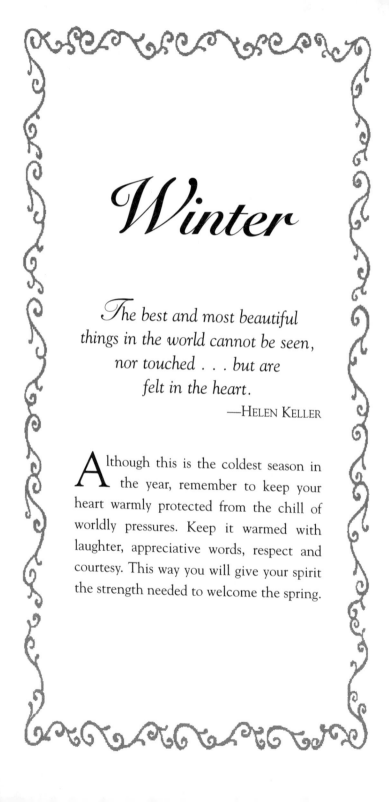

Winter

*The best and most beautiful
things in the world cannot be seen,
nor touched . . . but are
felt in the heart.*

—HELEN KELLER

Although this is the coldest season in the year, remember to keep your heart warmly protected from the chill of worldly pressures. Keep it warmed with laughter, appreciative words, respect and courtesy. This way you will give your spirit the strength needed to welcome the spring.

January

January 1

··

Deliberate Acts of Kindness for New Year's Day

New Year's Day is a great opportunity for renewal. Most of us respond to this holiday with hope and wishes for the positive changes we seek in our lives. New Year's resolutions are one way of trying to move oneself toward this renewal, toward a rebirth of spirit often seen as achievable through a change of habits. Perhaps the best way to change habits, however, is to change spirit first. Habits are supported by our values and the attitudes that enable them. If your spiritual commitment and understanding changes, it is likely that your habits will alter as well.

- If your habit at the new year is to make resolutions, ask yourself if you have usually been successful in living up to them. If so, continue. If not, perhaps you have been making unreasonable demands on yourself. An act of kindness to yourself would be to make more reasonable and achievable resolutions this year. Build success into them.

- Speaking of resolutions, you can engage in a mutual-assistance pact with a good friend or your spouse in which each agrees to help the other to live up to a resolution that you make this year. And one part of the aid is to help each other choose doable resolutions!

- This holiday is a perfect time to mend fences, make peace, get yourself straight with all your friends and family. Do you have a friend or cousin you haven't called or written in too long? Now's the time to call or write. Have a grudge? Decide to forgive and to let the other person know that things are cleared between you. Or make that apology now that you've avoided for so long.

- Write a letter of hopes and dreams for the new year. Spend some hours on it. Put it away for a day or two and then reread it. See if you'd like to let someone you love read it with you.

- Do a year-end review with your life partner or very good friend. Talk about your accomplishments and frustrations, achievements and missed opportunities during the past year. Then talk about your hopes and dreams for the coming year.

- Contribute your time, your money or your interest and concern to a charity of your choice. Make a place for this in your life this year.

January 2

....

*It is only with the heart that
one can see rightly, what is essential
is invisible to the eye.*

—Antoine de Saint-Exupéry

Our essential self, which we also call the soul, recognizes the value of other souls. If we could only see through all the distractions, the externals—how they dress, their ethnicity, how much they own, what school they've been to—which we've been so painstakingly taught to value, we would see right through to their essential selves and we'd find more love inside ourselves for those we meet. We are sometimes distracted and blinded by these things.

- Have you ever tuned in to how distanced from others we all are by nonessential things?

- Can you, just for today, decide to see other people through the innocent eyes of a child? And, if you did, how would that affect your day and your relationships with others?

- Take just one person, today, and decide to look past the quick judgments and responses we've all been trained to have. What do you see when you look at this person with your heart's invisible eye?

- How can you use this vision every day?

January 3

It pays to know the enemy—not least because at some time you may have the opportunity to turn him into a friend.

—Margaret Thatcher

_____

_____

_____

_____

_____

_____

_____

_____

_____

_____

_____

_____

_____

_____

_____

January 4

....

> *Where there is no truth,*
> *there is no kindness.*
>
> —Nachman of Bratslav

....

*He who brings up an orphan
is considered by Scripture as if he had
brought the child into being.*

—Ancient rabbinic saying

January 6

*Kindness is one of the most
attractive assets of the human race.
Therefore, as God's chosen people, holy
and dearly loved, clothe yourselves with
compassion, kindness, humility,
gentleness and patience.*

—Col. 3:12

_____
_____
_____
_____
_____
_____
_____
_____
_____
_____
_____
_____
_____
_____
_____
_____

January 7

*It is better for a man to be
thrown into a fiery furnace than to bring
another to shame in public.*

—Ketuboth

*Take care not to make pale
the face of another.*

—Baba Metzia

January 8

Shall we make a new rule of life from tonight: Always try to be a little kinder than is necessary?

—Sir James Matthew Barrie, *The Little White Bird*

What are the "minimums and maximums" of kindness? How kind is "just kind enough"? Sometimes, people come from a deficit mentality, believing that there are just so many things around to share, just so much love, or time, or attention or any other resource they need in life. We choose to come to each day of life from an abundance mentality, and by doing so, we see the world as full of the potential for love, caring, attention and sharing. We don't think that you can be "too kind." We don't let the fear of being taken advantage of stop us from reaching out in caring to others.

- How much of your behavior toward others is affected by a fear of being taken advantage of or of losing others' respect because you seem too nice?

- How much do you hold back warm feelings or the desire to reach out for fear of being seen as an overwhelming or controlling person?

- It is possible for you to find ways to express your kindest feelings and impulses without losing others' respect and your own safe boundaries?

- Just for today, try to go one step past your usual comfort zone in expressing your kindness in just one area of your life.

January 9

....

*N*ever love unless you can bear with all
the faults of Man.

—Thomas Campion, *The Third Book of Airs*, 1617

True kindness means being able to get past your judgments of others and accept them for who they are, "warts and all." We humans all have flaws. The biblical quote, "Judge not lest ye be judged," speaks to the heart of this idea.

- Do an inventory of the significant relationships in your life. List all the people who impact on you. Rank this list in terms of those with whom you feel you'd like to spend time or energy repairing, establishing, enriching or deepening your relationship. Use numbers from one to five.

- What does your list tell you about your values? Which of the people on your list seem to have flaws *similar to yours?*

- People often judge most harshly others who display traits they cannot forgive in themselves. Is this true for you to any degree?

- Integrate kindness more fully into your life this week by deciding to forgive two people for their faults, flaws, bad habits, inconsistencies: Forgive the other person and forgive yourself!

- Start small. Like someone b*ecause of* who they are, not *in spite of* it. Choose one little flaw and make the decision to accept it in someone, including yourself.

January 10
··

*Every charitable act is a stepping stone
towards heaven.*

—Henry Ward Beecher

_____

_____

_____

_____

_____

_____

_____

_____

_____

_____

_____

_____

_____

_____

_____

_____

_____

_____

January 11

....

*If you haven't got any charity
in your heart, you have the worst
kind of heart trouble.*

—Bob Hope

_____

_____

_____

_____

_____

_____

_____

_____

_____

_____

_____

_____

_____

_____

_____

_____

January 12

How excellent is thy loving-kindness, O God! Therefore the children of men put their trust under the shadow of thy wings.

—Psalm 36:7

January 13

*Love ye your enemies and do
good, and lend, hoping for nothing again;
and your reward shall be great, and
ye shall be the children of the Highest:
For he is kind unto the unthankful
and to the evil.*

—Luke 6:35

January 14

There once was a very wise
doctor who prescribed for his patients the
"Thank You Cure." He knew that often
his patients were plagued with the troubles
of the world and would come to him
with symptoms of stress, worry,
discouragement and fear. He told his
patients to express their appreciation
to their friends, family and everyone they
come in contact with who does them a
good turn or favor. Performing the
act of "thank you" requires a smile to get it
just right. As you might have guessed,
many of his patients expressed to him
that they really did feel better.

—Fred Bauer

....

Deliberate Acts of Kindness for Martin Luther King Day

We've got some difficult days ahead.
But it really doesn't matter with me now.
Because I've been to the mountain top.
Like anybody, I'd like to live a long life, [but]
I've seen the Promised Land. I may not
get there with you, [but] we as a people will get
[there]. . . . So I'm happy tonight. I'm not
fearing any man. Mine eyes have seen the
glory of the coming of the Lord.

—The Reverend Martin Luther King Jr.

The Reverend Martin Luther King Jr. was a tireless fighter for equal rights and for the extension of the full freedoms of our country to every citizen, no matter their color or national origin. Like all human beings, he had his flaws and imperfections. Unlike most of us, however, he had that special brand of courage to risk his life to achieve his dream. Even those who disagreed with him had to acknowledge his courage and commitment to his cause.

What do you believe in enough to risk your job, your reputation, your friendships or your life? Most of us live our lives in the mundane world of everyday chores, habits and responsibilities. We seek the weekend pleasures and the safety of a secure job. Our advance thinking, if we do any, is likely to be about long-term purchases such as a big vacation, that house in the country, the power boat we've dreamed of owning. People like the Reverend Martin Luther King Jr. have a bigger and loftier vision to which they dedicate their lives: the improvement of some dimension of life for everyone. Leaders of movements are special people indeed, because they point out to us that our lives can have a larger purpose and a greater meaning. Mother Teresa of Calcutta, John Muir, Mahatma Gandhi and others remind us that there can be more to life than getting that third TV set.

What does MLK Day mean to you? How can its message become significant in your life?

- Write a letter to an elected official or to a news-paper about an issue you are concerned about. Take a stand. Be fearless and full of integrity.

- Call in to an angry, negatively focused talk show with a positive statement about America. Or tell them that you'd appreciate them finding what's right about our country rather than fomenting dissatisfaction and more hatred. Be prepared for their contempt and to be hung up on.

- Find a way to acknowledge, value and/or celebrate the people you live near or work with who are different from you. Remember that this country's greatness comes from its remarkable blend of people from every culture on the planet. Our uniqueness is in our empowering and blending of differences, not in our homogenization.

January 16

*The happiness of life is made up of
minute fractions—the little soon forgotten
charities of a kiss or smile, a kind look,
a heartfelt compliment, and the countless
infinistesimals of pleasurable
and genial feeling.*

—Samuel Taylor Coleridge, *The Friend*

Kindness does not have to be showy, spectacular, costly or even time-consuming. For many people, the kindnesses that make life most bearable are the very little ones, the daily sweet acts done almost unconsciously by those whose habits are kind.

- Think back in your life to a little kind word or kind act you received that may have taken the giver only a moment, but became a lifetime memory for you. Write one or two of these down. Share them with someone.

- As you think of small kindnesses from your past, what sorts of feelings do you experience?

- Small kindnesses come in many flavors: a kind word; the quick, uncalculating offer of a helping hand to someone struggling with a bundle; a pat on the back to a clerk who helps you in a store. What others can you think of?

- Carry a notepad today and jot down all the small kindnesses you see around you. Resolve to add to the list through your own small kindnesses tomorrow.

January 17

*There are three rules of dealing
with those who come to us (1) Kindness,
(2) Kindness, (3) Kindness.*

—Bishop Fulton Sheen

_____

_____

_____

_____

_____

_____

_____

_____

_____

_____

_____

_____

_____

_____

_____

January 18

We cannot make the kingdom
of God happen, but . . . we can be kind
to each other. We can be kind to ourselves. We can drive back the darkness a
little. We can make green places within
ourselves where God can make
his kingdom happen.

—Frederick Buechner

_____

_____

_____

_____

_____

_____

_____

_____

_____

_____

_____

_____

_____

_____

January 19

Be kind and merciful.
Let no one ever come to you without
leaving better and happier. Be the living
express of God's kindness: kindness in
your face, kindness in your eyes, kindness
in your smile, kindness in your warm
greeting. In the slums we are the light of
God's kindness to the poor. To children, to
the poor, to all who suffer and are lonely,
give always a happy smile. Give them
not only your care, but your heart.

—Mother Teresa

January 20

We have a deep and abiding hunger
for a refreshing sight of goodness and courage
and kindness to renew our faith in ourselves
and in one another. So much of our
contemporary literature betrays our human
possibilities because it is forever focusing on
the meanness of man, the sordid, the animal.
The popular novel moves alternately between
the bedroom and the jungle. It is true of
course as has been said, that the heart
of man is often a cesspool, but just as often
it is a sanctuary, and to forget either one
is to create a caricature. It also fails to
nourish our hunger for evidence of
human nobility which can elicit
the best within ourselves.

—Sidney Greenberg, *Hidden Hungers*

January 21

*All values in this world are more
or less questionable, but the most important
thing in life is human kindness.*

—Suzanne Simon

_____

_____

_____

_____

_____

_____

_____

_____

_____

_____

_____

_____

_____

_____

_____

_____

_____

_____

_____

_____

_____

January 22

*Live your life as though there
is great joy to be experienced around each
curve in the road, an abundance of
goodness in each person you come in
contact with and the knowledge that you
have enough inner wisdom to answer
the mysteries that challenge you.*

—Meladee McCarty

A great act of kindness is to take a leap of faith and decide to trust yourself, to believe that you do have inner wisdom. Accept yourself for who you are and forgive yourself for the imperfections, errors, mistakes and failures that are inevitable for all humans. Despite these flaws, you know that you have a basic goodness, a lot of talent and ability, and that the direction you are taking will ultimately prove to be useful and productive in important ways. If you can make this decision and take on this faith in yourself, you will certainly reap these benefits: You'll be less likely to be swayed by others, you'll have a greater sense of purpose and you'll be much less dependent on so-called experts. You are, after all, the only true expert on your own life. And you will have to live with the consequences while the advice-givers go home "scot-free."

*As long as I have to die my own death,
I have decided to live my own life and
not let others live it for me.*

—Hanoch McCarty

- Think of a time when you were torn between what others were advising you to do and what your own intuition said to do. How did you resolve this? What happened to your sense of self and your feeling of peace when this happened?

- Today is a day to affirm yourself, your power and potential, your accomplishments and even the courage that it took to do those things that may have ended as failures. You are a human, with all the glory and possibilities that implies. You have a loving spirit that cannot be denied. Allow it free rein for just this day.

January 23

Each of us has a teddy bear and
a grizzly bear inside along with a bunch of
other selves which come out at
the oddest moments.

—Hanoch McCarty

Always have a smile, a laugh and a
hug to give.

—Stephanie Dodds

At what times does your "teddy bear" self come out and what provokes your "grizzly bear" to start growling at others? Are there certain kinds of events that trigger the negative side of your personality? Do you feel as though you are in control of this? I saw a couple who were having a shouting match, snarling and hissing invectives at each other. The phone rang and the woman answered it. "Oh, nothing, everything is fine," she said sweetly. I couldn't believe my ears. The conversation went on for several minutes and she was able to sound as sweet, positive and relaxed as could be. As soon as she got off the phone, she continued with the argument, her anger unabated. Could she say that she was out of control?

- Somewhere, deep inside you, is there a control center that really decides when to unleash your grizzly bear?

- What is the balance between teddy bear and grizzly bear moments in your life? Are you happy with that balance? How can you change it if you want to?

- Are there other aspects of your true self besides the two bears? What are they and when do they appear?

January 24

. . . .

*If we see a hungry man, who is
so callous that he will not give him a piece
of bread? But all around us people are
starving and we do not have the time or
the thoughtfulness or the compassion
to speak a kind word, perform a gracious
act, make a call, drop a line, to give
bread to emaciated spirits.*

—Hartmore House

. . . .

Bitter are the tears of a child:
Sweeten them.
Deep are the thoughts of a child:
Quiet them.
Sharp is the grief of a child:
Take it from him.
Soft is the heart of a child:
Do not harden it.

—Pamela Glenconner

_____

_____

_____

_____

_____

_____

_____

_____

_____

_____

_____

_____

January 26

If a child is to keep alive his inborn sense of wonder, he needs the companionship of at least one adult who can share it, rediscovering with him the joy, excitement and mystery of the world we live in.

—Rachel Carson

*Parenthood remains the greatest single
preserve of the amateur.*

—Alvin Toffler

January 28
....

*To bring up a child in the
way he should go, travel that way
yourself once in a while.*

—Josh Billings

_____

_____

_____

_____

_____

_____

_____

_____

_____

_____

_____

_____

_____

_____

_____

_____

_____

_____

January 29

....

If I'm too kind, I risk seeming
vulnerable or weak. Or maybe I'll be expected
to do the same things again and again.
Being kind can have some drawbacks.

—Anonymous

There are many fears that prevent people from doing acts of kindness: the fear of seeming weak, the fear of being taken advantage of, the fear of being sued, even a fear of the expense of time or money which may be involved. Consider that the urge to do kindness comes from a deep and authentic part of your spirit. Yet we can be tormented by fears and second thoughts that conflict with our more open and giving self. How you resolve this conflict will speak to you loudly about who you are and how well you judge yourself. Finding the courage to be kind and to overcome these doubts is one key to a more peaceful inner life.

- Think about the doubts and fears that occur to you when considering an act of kindness. Take the time to write them in your journal. You may be surprised as you begin writing, that more will occur to you than you imagined.

- Review your list and ask yourself how many of these concerns have a basis in fact. Did any of these doubts come true? Draw a line through any of them that you think are only fantasies and not based on your experience.

- Consider now those that are left. You've had, perhaps, some negative experiences that taught you to fear being kind in certain circumstances. Can you decide that they, in fact, teach a different lesson instead? Write about what that lesson might be.

January 30

I discovered I always have choices and sometimes it's only a choice of attitude.

—Judith M. Knowlton

Being kind to others is not always easy. Doing kind acts for pleasant, cheery people who you know will reciprocate by showing you gratitude is "safe." Sometimes, however, we must choose to be kind even though others are not kind to us. Often, these people are hurting inside and need our kindness. By changing our attitude about others who appear unkind, we have the ability to bring out the best in ourselves and others.

- Can you think of an incident in which you were treated rudely? How did you feel? What was your reaction?
- How might you have handled the situation differently? Do you think the outcome would have changed? Write about it in your journal.

January 31

What lies behind us and lies before us
are small matters compared to what lies
within us.

—Ralph Waldo Emerson

February

Deliberate Acts of Kindness for Presidents' Day
(Third Monday in February)

*I believe that every human mind
feels pleasure in doing good to another.*

—Thomas Jefferson

Our most quoted, most admired presidents seem to have been those who consistently refocused us on our most positive values, not those who continually retreated to a crowd-pleasing jingoism. A president's greatest authority is his moral force, the ability to remind us of the best that is in us, of those values we most highly prize and cherish.

If Washington did or didn't actually throw the silver dollar across a river or if it is eventually proved that the cherry-tree-chopping story is just a fable, we want to find in our highest leaders a spiritual center that is free from decay. This person whom we have communally raised to high office represents to us something powerful about ourselves. If we see our president's values as decayed or suspect, we lose a sense of our own worth. Conversely, when we see this person as admirable, we become more so as well.

- Which president, or presidents, have had the most positive impact on your life? Write about this in your journal.

- On this Presidents' Day, write a letter to a young person you know, even your own child, about your thoughts on the role that presidents play as a model of our higher aspirations as a nation.

- Write a letter to the editor of your local newspaper with a positive story about one of our presidents or about some well-known political leader. Make sure to focus on this person's best qualities. As people read this, especially children, you will have the effect of bringing them hope for their country.

- Volunteer to dress up as one of the "Founding Fathers" and tell stories during the week of Presidents' Day in a local elementary school or public library.

February 1
....

> *P*leasant words are as
> an honeycomb, sweet to the soul,
> and health to the bones.
>
> —Prov. 16:24

Words have a powerful effect on the way we see "reality." Choosing to use absolute words like *always* and *never* puts tight limits on our possibilities. Other language lays blame or avoids responsibility: "You made me feel _____." "I have to _____." "I should _____." The so-called reality we experience when we choose these words is a sour one indeed—a world of unpleasant obligation and victimhood. It is possible to choose a powerful language, words that speak of your power to choose and your ability to make a difference in your own and in others' lives. Instead of "I have to," you substitute "I get to." Instead of "I should," you say, "I choose to." There's a pitiful whininess in the first set of words and an admirable and courageous strength in the second.

- Have you ever felt that someone's words affected how you feel and how you behave? Write about that in your journal.

- In what ways would your choosing words that take ownership of your feelings and your actions be a kindness to others?

- "If you can't say something positive, say nothing at all." How do you feel about this idea?

February 2

···

*Love looks through a telescope; envy
through a microscope.*

—Josh Billings

Love, on both romantic and humanitarian levels, is
large in scope. It is far-reaching and all-inclusive. It
is macroscopic.

Envy, on the other hand, is microscopic. This
emotion causes us to unfairly examine every detail of
another's life. When we are envious, we often falsely
pick apart a person's reputation and character. It makes
us feel tight and withdrawn; love expands our universe,
opens us up and allows us to "breathe" in the best.

- Can you think of a time when you were envious of
  someone? What did you do? How did you feel?

- Rethink the situation and write down in your
  journal how being happy for the person might
  have changed your feelings.

February 3

The first duty of love is to listen.

—Paul Tillich

· ·

All children alarm their parents,
if only because you are forever expecting
to encounter yourself.

—Gore Vidal

_____

_____

_____

_____

_____

_____

_____

_____

_____

_____

_____

_____

_____

_____

_____

February 5

··

> *Example is not the main thing in influencing others. It is the only thing.*
>
> —Albert Schweitzer

_____

_____

_____

_____

_____

_____

_____

_____

_____

_____

_____

_____

_____

_____

_____

_____

February 6

....

*You grow up the first time you
laugh at yourself.*

—Ethel Barrymore

_____

_____

_____

_____

_____

_____

_____

_____

_____

_____

_____

_____

_____

_____

_____

_____

_____

February 7

We are all capable of everything.

—Virgil

_____

_____

_____

_____

_____

_____

_____

_____

_____

_____

_____

_____

_____

_____

_____

_____

_____

_____

February 8

∙∙∙

*I believe it is the nature of people to
be heroes, given a chance.*

—J.A. Autry

There are so many people who have lived through intense pain and deep hurt who have transcended those experiences and chosen to express kindness, compassion or forgiveness when it would be so simple and understandable if they were bitter, closed, suspicious or uncaring. What caused people during the Holocaust to hide Jewish children or to share their last crust of bread? Victor Frankl, himself a survivor of the camps, said that it was the choice to share with others that established the humanity of the giver and rendered him free in spirit if he couldn't be free physically. By self-sacrifice, the giver attains the power of decision-making and of moral wholeness.

- You are called upon to express your heroism by letting go of pain, hurt or anger, no matter how justified. When you think about that, what comes up for you? Which of your experiences most need transcending?

- Our most negative feelings can be so strong *and so addictive*, that we become enslaved by them. We've seen people trapped in cycles of anger, hurt, revenge and victimhood, playing out the same story endlessly. Can you see how freeing it would be to let go of these feelings? Write in your journal about the power you would attain if you could let go in this way.

February 9

··

> *Let me live in my house by the side of
> the road and be a friend to man.*
>
> —Old proverb

"Live and let live" can be interpreted as an injunction to take care of oneself and no others or as a plan to take care of one's own life and to be caring and respectful of others. It is the deepest, most profound decision, to choose a life of kindness, of being involved in mankind in the specific sense of one's daily behavior to neighbors, family and friends.

- Our neighbor, Freddy Gudel, climbs on his tractor and mows the highway frontage by his property. He could, we suppose, just stop there and go on to his next task, but, instead he takes the extra 15 minutes to come down the road and do the grass in front of our place, too. Have you known people like Freddy in your life? Write down their names, and beside them, write some of their kind acts to mankind.

- Write a note to one person on your list and thank him or her, saying what those kind acts meant to you.

- Take something you're planning today, anything, and see if you can imagine a way to extend it so it benefits others. Now plan that out. Imagine doing it that way. How will that feel?

- Do we create the world, one act at a time? Can you build into your daily life this idea of extending your plans to include benefit to others? This acts out the phrase, "Think globally, act locally."

February 10

*Love is an act of endless forgiveness,
a tender look which becomes habit.*

—Peter Ustinov

February 11

....

*People come together because they need
each other and they need to hear victories
about each other.*

—Bill Milliken

_____

_____

_____

_____

_____

_____

_____

_____

_____

_____

_____

_____

_____

_____

_____

_____

February 12

*Parents were invented to
make children happy by giving them
something to ignore.*

—Ogden Nash

_____

_____

_____

_____

_____

_____

_____

_____

_____

_____

_____

_____

_____

_____

_____

_____

_____

February 13

··

> *Hope is the feeling you have that the feeling you have isn't permanent.*
>
> —Jean Kerr

_____

_____

_____

_____

_____

_____

_____

_____

_____

_____

_____

_____

_____

_____

_____

_____

February 14

....

Deliberate Acts of Kindness
for Valentine's Day

Thoughts:

Valentine's Day is a sweet celebration of love and of relationships worth nurturing. Many holidays have come far from their roots and origins, and this is a good example. Today we approach this holiday in a light-hearted way—as an opportunity to express affection or to show romantic interest. Children give valentines to their teachers, and parents give them to their children. It is a day for showing you care. While there is a strong romantic element to the day, many people do express simple affection (without the romance) or appreciation to a wide variety of others in their lives.

- One of the problems, on this as well as other holidays, is to find a card that expresses just the right amount of feeling for its intended recipient. If you're choosing a card for your secretary, can you find one that expresses appreciation without conveying the idea of romantic interest? If you're sending a card to someone you've just started dating, can you find a card that expresses interest without overwhelming and seeming to go too far too fast? Many people use humorous cards for this purpose. What has been your experience with this issue?

- Valentine's Day, which had its beginnings as a saint's day, has been transformed in America. Its celebration of love, especially romantic love, can be a delight if you are involved in a loving relationship, or it can be threatening and depressing if you are not. What feelings are raised in you by this day?

- Can you remember your childhood celebrations of Valentine's Day? What were they like?

Actions:

- Create a "valentine-making kit" out of red construction paper, lacy paper doilies, glue and envelopes, and help your children create valentines for their friends and family members. Remind them to include family members they may not see very often and classmates who may not be popular and who may get few cards from anyone.

- You can get your valentine's card postmarked from a romantic location with a little bit of advance work:

  a) Pick your card and seal it in a stamped envelope addressed to your love.

  b) Place it inside a larger envelope that is addressed to the postmaster of the town you choose from the list below. Add a note asking for the card to be hand-stamped with the local postmark.

  c) Mail it well in advance so there's time to process it. Remember that these postmasters will get a lot of similar requests.

Valentine, NE 69201	Romance, WV 25175
Loveland, CO 80537	Loving, NM 88256
Valentine, TX 79854	Kissimmee, FL 32741

- Hide little candy hearts all over your loved one's things—in suit pockets, suitcases, closets, car dashboard—everywhere.

- Send a valentine of appreciation to all those on whom you depend: your secretary, your most trusted co-worker, your best neighbor.

February 15

· ·

*Why do back rubs always
become front rubs? We need to learn
to see the difference between
sensuality and sexuality.*

—Sidney B. Simon

If you don't cuddle, you'll curdle.

—Jess Lair

You know the story: The husband begins by offering his wife a tender backrub. Delighted, she agrees and relaxes gratefully as loving hands help remove pains and aches earned by a long day's work. The feel of his wife's body under his hands, his deep love for her and his own sexual needs combine. He becomes increasingly aroused. Almost without plan, his hands wander away from her back and shoulders and onto her breasts. What began as a tender offer of massage becomes sex. Certainly we are not against sex, and this scenario may be just fine with both participants. But we'd like you to think about the idea that perhaps the other partner wasn't in the mood for sex at this moment. Maybe, just maybe, he or she was really too tired, too achy, too low in energy. This leads us to several acts of kindness:

- being clear about your intentions with your partner;
- communicating your needs openly; and, most important,

- being capable of giving *just plain pure cuddles, cuddles that are guaranteed not to lead anywhere else*, cuddles that your partner can fully relax into.

- What has been your experience with the confusion between sensuality (cuddles and caring) and sexuality? Does it mirror the story we told? How does it make you feel?

- What would it be like to be in a non-exploitive relationship characterized by mutual respect and caring? Are you in one right now? What can you do to move your closest relationship toward that ideal?

- Are there any other areas in relationships, beside cuddling/sexuality, in which best intentions end up astray?

February 16

Lean on me.

—Anonymous

It's okay to ask for help. You don't have to solve every problem and bear every burden alone. Our society places an enormous emphasis on self-reliance and individual accomplishment. Each is a worthy trait, but we also need to cut ourselves and others a little slack— give permission to need, to request, to accept help. And it is good when we can offer help in ways that do not demean the other's sense of worth.

- Most Americans report that they find it much easier to offer help than to accept it. How about you? Can you be a receiver when you need it? Can you calm that insistent inner voice that tells you to go it alone?

- One problem with giving or accepting help is how to prevent it from becoming a dependency. Give some thought today to how you can keep your helping process healthy. Write down your ideas.

- One avenue toward healthy kindness is to try to keep it in balance. Being always the giver is not balanced, nor is being always the taker. We need to strive for reciprocity in our relationships. How are you dealing with this today?

- It sometimes helps to become aware of the sources of these ideas in your life. From whom did you learn your attitudes about giving and taking? Are those attitudes still working for you?

February 17

··

People should think less about what they
ought to do and more about what they
ought to be. If only their living were good,
their work would shine forth brightly.

—Meister Eckhart

_____

_____

_____

_____

_____

_____

_____

_____

_____

_____

_____

_____

_____

_____

_____

_____

_____

February 18

....

I don't know the key to
success but the key to failure is trying
to please everybody.

—Bill Cosby

_____

_____

_____

_____

_____

_____

_____

_____

_____

_____

_____

_____

_____

_____

_____

_____

_____

_____

_____

_____

February 19

....

*If you've never been hated by
your child, you've never been a parent.*

—Bette Davis

February 20

Forgiveness is a way we can alter
the past.

—David Bella

February 21

....

> *M*aterial abundance without character
> is the surest way to destruction.

—Thomas Jefferson

February 22

....

*Talk of wasted affections; affection
never was wasted.*

—Henry Wadsworth Longfellow

We give of our time and our love; we extend a kindness and the gesture is not appreciated, nor is it returned. We are tempted to believe that it was wasted. You find "just the right shirt" for your son, away at college. With delight, you wrap and mail it. Then the long wait to see if he received it. No call. No letter. No thank-you. You get discouraged, thinking your act of kindness wasn't appreciated. So was the affection wasted? We think not. Kindness gives something of value to the giver and the receiver. Even though the receiver ought to respond, he or she usually does feel gratitude and gains the use of whatever was sent.

- How do you feel about this? Have you experience with gifts sent and not responded to appropriately?

- Have you taught your children (if you have any) to write thank-you notes? Is today the day to begin? Have you modeled this for them? Ask your children if they have ever given a gift or done a kindness that was not acknowledged and how they felt.

- Some people will respond to their gifts and kindnesses being ignored by striking that person off the list and never sending or giving again. How do you feel about this response? What will the consequences be for their relationships?

- How would our world be affected if people chose Policy A (forgive the non-responder and keep sending gifts, doing kindnesses) or Policy B (strike 'em off the list, forget them, nurse a hurt feeling)? Which policy do you think is healthier for the world you'd like to live in?

February 23

I don't get mad, I get even.

—T-shirt slogan

*R*evenge is sweet.

—Old saying

*A*n eye for an eye, a tooth for a tooth,
a brother for a brother, vengeance
is mine saith the Lord.

—The Bible

The urge for revenge is one of man's oldest companions. It would be foolish to deny the power of this urge in most of us. Many people, when slighted, engage in elaborate and protracted revenge fantasies and in threatening talk. Others don't stop at mere fantasy but move on to vengeful actions. We think that most revenge isn't shown on TV news, it is far more subtle and pervasive. For example, revenge is being forgetful—never remembering something your "enemy" wants or needs. Revenge is constant lateness, or slowness or the pretense of stupidity. "It's not my job," says the vengeful clerk, hating the job and everyone who comes to the counter. "I don't know where that is, you'll have to wait until Mr. Schmenge comes back from vacation." Revenge is delighting in someone else's failures or misfortunes. It is also expressed by those who enforce rules and procedures in needlessly strict and rigid interpretations.

- Has revenge "worked for you" in your life? Has revenge brought you relief from anger or hurt without also bringing other negative consequences to you?

- We think that it takes much courage and hard work to make the choice to sidestep the urge for revenge; to choose to be loving or at the least, work on forgiveness. Would it be worth it, do you think? What would be the benefits to you?

- Our world is filled with examples of revenge cycles gone crazy; feuds and wars between ethnic, racial or religious groups often fill the headlines. Is there any action that you can take to help the world move away from the revenge cycle? How about in the way you train your children? Or in the example you set to friends and family?

February 24

....

*Self-confidence is the first requisite
to great undertakings.*

—Samuel Johnson

_____

_____

_____

_____

_____

_____

_____

_____

_____

_____

_____

_____

_____

_____

_____

_____

_____

_____

_____

February 25

....

*The shoe that fits one person
pinches another; there is no recipe for
living that suits all cases.*

—Carl Jung

_____

_____

_____

_____

_____

_____

_____

_____

_____

_____

_____

_____

_____

_____

_____

_____

_____

_____

February 26

··

No answer is also an answer.

—German proverb

_____

_____

_____

_____

_____

_____

_____

_____

_____

_____

_____

_____

_____

_____

_____

_____

February 27

··

One never notices what has been done; one can only see what remains to be done.

—Marie Curie

February 28

....

*W*e pardon to the extent that we love.

—François duc de La Rochefoucauld

_____

_____

_____

_____

_____

_____

_____

_____

_____

_____

_____

_____

_____

_____

_____

_____

_____

_____

March

March 1

....

> *Kindness is for wimps.*
> *What are you, some kind of airheaded*
> *do-gooder? Do you think that you're*
> *Mother Teresa? If I behaved the way you*
> *suggest, people would use me*
> *as a doormat!*
>
> —Drive-time DJ, Miami, March 1994

To be kind runs the risk of being seen as soft, vulnerable, foolish. In an age of cynicism and self-interest, you will stand out. Those who revile you probably secretly admire and envy you. They may wish they had the courage to behave like you. Kindness takes a unique sort of courage: the courage of conviction. To be kind is to admit that you actually believe in something. It may be more popular to seem cool and uncaring, disengaged, distant, uninvolved. The kind person is often a pioneer, showing others the alternatives to indifference and selfishness.

- Has it taken courage to be kind at any time in your life? Think of some examples and write them in your journal.

- Do you see a difference between active, planned, deliberate kindness and being a wimpy, soft-hearted and soft-headed fool?

- To be kind when others are choosing not to be takes considerable courage. Some would consider it a foolish and risky choice. What do you think?

March 2

....

Stupid is as stupid does, sir!

—Forrest Gump

In the movie, *Forrest Gump*, Tom Hanks plays a man whose intelligence is quite limited. It's clear that he is developmentally handicapped, yet people keep teasing and baiting him. Children stone him, chase him, torture him. Why are some people mean?

Meanness is a learned trait. With some it's a habit; with others, a hobby. There are those who have never been taught compassion or empathy. The almost universal childhood curiosity that leads children to mistreat animals, "just to see what they would do," is usually tempered by empathy as we grow older. This tempering process is stimulated by a caring adult who teaches us by lesson and by example to care about other people's and other creatures' feelings and well-being. Consider those who grow up in homes that have no wise adult model like this. Other people may have had this early training but perhaps a series of disasters, misfortunes or tragedies left them feeling like wounded birds. Wounded birds will peck your hand if you try to help them. Their pain is so great that they cannot see your helping hand as anything but a threat. People who act as wounded birds hurt others because the fact that someone *isn't* hurting as they do frightens or angers them.

- How can you help a wounded bird? The first step is to gather up all your good intent—your energy must be fully mobilized, because wounded birds take a lot of work to reach. The second step is to remind yourself that hurt and angry people are likely to be ungrateful, even actively hostile, toward the very person who is trying to help. Are you ready to help a wounded bird today?

• Dealing with hurt and angry people requires different skills and behaviors from the usual. For example, you will have to be totally honest about your feelings. When a person lashes out at you, instead of retreating, ignoring or pretending that it didn't hurt, it's much more effective to say, "I felt hurt when you said that. Did you intend to hurt me?" "I get angry when you choose to do (or say) things like that. I would really like you to stop." Can you be so direct?

• Can you see the kindness in all this confrontation? The kindness is that who you are and how you feel *can be trusted*. And that you are giving the person straight feedback on how they have to change in order to be accepted. And you are facing them with the consequences of their actions. As tough as it sounds, this is truly kindness. Write in your journal your thoughts on this.

March 3

....

*Loving is not just looking at each other,
it's looking in the same direction.*

—Antoine de Saint-Exupéry

_____

_____

_____

_____

_____

_____

_____

_____

_____

_____

_____

_____

_____

_____

_____

_____

March 4

....

> The fundamental defect of
> fathers is that they want their children
> to be a credit to them.
>
> —Bertrand Russell

_____

_____

_____

_____

_____

_____

_____

_____

_____

_____

_____

_____

_____

_____

_____

_____

March 5

....

*People who fight fire with fire
usually end up with ashes.*

—Abigail Van Buren

_____

_____

_____

_____

_____

_____

_____

_____

_____

_____

_____

_____

_____

_____

_____

_____

March 6
....

If you scatter thorns, don't go barefoot.

—Italian proverb

_____

_____

_____

_____

_____

_____

_____

_____

_____

_____

_____

_____

_____

_____

_____

_____

_____

March 7

....

*There are victories of the
soul and spirit. Sometimes, even if
you lose, you win.*

—Elie Wiesel

_____

_____

_____

_____

_____

_____

_____

_____

_____

_____

_____

_____

_____

_____

_____

_____

_____

_____

March 8

....

> *I can't help myself,*
> *I'm just that kind of a person.*
>
> —Anonymous

You have met or will meet someone who uses language like this to give themselves permission to do something harmful to themselves or others. "I'm quick-tempered. That's just how I am. So I blew up and let you have it. Sorry. You'll have to forgive me. I've always been that way." The little shrug that accompanies this kind of talk completes it. You see, the person isn't responsible for themselves or their actions. The comedian Flip Wilson had a comic character, Geraldine, who always said, with a sly smile, "The Devil made me do it!" And this was used to explain away anything.

It is an act of kindness and courage to resolve to stop excusing away inappropriate or hateful behavior. Just because you "always did it that way" doesn't mean that you have to go on doing it. Today is the day and now is the time for change. If you are the recipient of the behavior, you can ask, "Did you enjoy what you just did? Are you aware that it hurt me? I would like you to stop." If you are the perpetrator, it's time to own your behavior and all its consequences.

- Do you know anyone who gives themselves a "license to be dysfunctional" in this way? What do they say or do that excuses their behavior? How do you feel when this happens?

- Can you think of any times when you have done this, too? When were they?

- All human beings have faults, blind spots, things we don't do particularly well or gracefully. If, however, we decide "that's just how we are," we foreclose the possibility of growth or positive change. You will meet people who have given up on themselves and do not believe that they can grow any further. How about you? What do you believe?

March 9

∙∙∙

> *Not he who has much is rich,*
> *but he who gives much.*
>
> —Erich Fromm

Our great friend Sidney Simon often discusses what he calls "enough-hood" in his personal growth workshops. How do you know when you have enough? Enough of anything: food, money, possessions, etc. How much is enough? What does having things mean to you? There's a T-shirt slogan we've seen that says, "Whoever has the most toys when he dies, wins." Is that what life is about? We think that riches can be measured by many yardsticks. How many people you love and who love you, how many acts of kindness you are remembered for when you are gone. As each day progresses, we are presented with new opportunities, most of which are invisible, to do our kind work in the world. For us, these moments, when seized and enjoyed to the fullest, leave us feeling fulfilled, content.

- When you were a child, what did you think "rich" meant? Have you changed much in your definition? What experiences changed you?

- If you were to learn that you are dying and have only one month of life left to you, what actions would you take? How many of them qualify as *acts of kindness?* Make a list of these actions.

- Now you've learned that the "diagnosis" was in error, you have a reprieve. Your normal lifespan, whatever it may be, has been restored to you. Look at your list again. How many actions will you commit to do in this coming month?

March 10

....

*Liberty is the only thing you can't have
unless you give it to others.*

—William Allen White

_____

_____

_____

_____

_____

_____

_____

_____

_____

_____

_____

_____

_____

_____

_____

_____

_____

March 11

··

*We can scare ourselves or
inspire ourselves. . . . We are the architects
of our own attitudes and experiences.
We design the world by the way
we choose to see it.*

—Barry Neil Kaufman

March 12

....

*The willingness to accept responsibility
for one's own life is the source from
which self-respect springs.*

—Joan Didion

_____

_____

_____

_____

_____

_____

_____

_____

_____

_____

_____

_____

_____

_____

_____

March 13

....

Do as the heavens have done,
forget your evil;
With them forgive yourself.

—William Shakespeare

_____

_____

_____

_____

_____

_____

_____

_____

_____

_____

_____

_____

_____

_____

_____

_____

March 14

....

*A great number of people think
they are thinking when they are merely
rearranging their prejudices.*

—William James

_____

_____

_____

_____

_____

_____

_____

_____

_____

_____

_____

_____

_____

_____

_____

March 15

....

> *Not buying into people's excuses*
> *can be an act of kindness. Insist, gently of*
> *course, that people be the best they can be.*
> *Refuse to accept shoddiness, half-done*
> *jobs, "just good enough" and other*
> *pretenses. Refuse to accept the 300*
> *reasons why it can't be done and ask if*
> *there are any reasons that it can be done.*
>
> —Hanoch McCarty

During World War I, there were artillery battles of incredible proportions. In the battle of Ypres, for example, over 500,000 shells were fired *per hour!* Often, entire regiments were wiped out with little trace. The horror was truly beyond description. Young men on both sides suffered from what was then called "shell shock." It was believed that the concussion was the cause of strange behavior that was noted in some of the soldiers. Later, in World War II, it was called "battle fatigue," and in the Vietnam War it was called Post-Traumatic Stress Disorder.

Back in 1915, German soldiers returning from the front would sometimes seem to behave in odd or frightening ways. Because of the danger of bad publicity, it was decided to try to help these men by giving them a special document that read something like, *Not responsible for his behavior. Return this man to his home or his Army unit. Shell shock victim.* In that way, a decorated hero would not be subject to arrest and the associated bad headlines, if he did something untoward in public. It isn't too hard to see, then, why a black market developed for these certificates! If you had one, you could get away with close to anything! In slang they were known as "crazy licenses."

Today, people get crazy licenses all the time. A crazy license is granted when you seem to have permission to do something that is unhealthy, unkind or uncaring. Other people will make excuses for you. "Of course, she didn't mean it when she said that. But you see, she had a death in the family recently." "Sure Bill is overeating and drinking too much but . . ."

- A courageous kindness is to gently but firmly revoke all crazy licenses and insist that people be responsible for their own behavioral choices.

- What would happen to you if you did that? Would you lose the friendship? Do you value the friend enough to risk the relationships?

- How can you do this in a way that will not sound like you've appointed yourself judge, jury and executioner?

March 16

....

*Though I speak with the tongues
of men and angels, and have not charity,
I am become as sounding brass,
or tinkling cymbal.*

—1 Cor. 13:1-3

We've heard the phrase, "a Hollywood invitation," which translates as an invitation that isn't really meant. Occasionally people offer a kindness that they hope you won't accept. "If there's anything I can do to help, don't hesitate to ask." Once we heard that said to someone whose house was ransacked by a burglar. Everything was strewn about, many items smashed. The person making the offer could have simply picked up a broom and started sweeping. But the offer was made in the act of leaving!

- How many Hollywood invitations have you received? Can you think of one that particularly rankled?

- Truth to tell, how many Hollywood invitations have you given? What were the reasons? (We're sure you have good ones.)

- How can we make our offers of kindness more genuine, immediate, concrete so that they are believable and believed?

- When unmeant offers are made, each person in hearing of them loses just that little bit of faith in the world. How much can you contribute to the restoration of people's faith in each other?

March 17

....

Deliberate Acts of Kindness
for St. Patrick's Day

Thoughts:

St. Patrick's Day is a unique holiday in the American calendar. No other ethnic holiday seems to have captured the American imagination as has this day. Everyone seems to be wearing green and claiming some Irish ancestry. It has its own parade—even in towns that have a 90 percent Swedish population, the St. Patty's Day Parade goes on year after year.

This is a day that evokes a smile from almost everyone and which brings to mind the mischievousness of leprechauns and the gaiety of Irish songs.

St. Patrick was kidnapped and enslaved by the Irish as a youth. Making his way back to England, he took religious vows and returned to Ireland to serve as a missionary to the very people who had enslaved him. St. Patrick forgave his captors and spent his life doing good works among the Irish clans and tribes.

- What sort of feelings do you have about St. Patrick's Day? Do you associate the holiday with any pleasant memories? Share those memories with a young member of your family.

- Invite your friends and family to a St. Patty's Day party. Serve the traditional corned beef and cabbage dinner, complete with green beer. Make copies of lots of old Irish songs and turn the evening into a sing-along. If you can, secure a flat drum similar to an Irish *bodhrán* and ask if any of your guests can play the pennywhistle or the flute, to accompany your crowd of eager singers. Get some recordings of the many Irish folk songs.

- Hire an Irish folk singer to come to your party and entertain. Make sure you've been clear that you expect the folk singer to be comfortable with people singing along.

- Contribute to charity in the name of St. Patrick.

- Bring a St. Patrick's Day celebration to someone who cannot get there independently. For example, recruit a group of your friends and bring all the traditional foods and party decorations to a group home, a retirement home, the home of a bed-ridden invalid.

- Invite your young children to study St. Patrick's life with you. Visit the library and see what you can find. Do this as a historical study rather than as a religious event. Discover what is known about this saint's life and ask your children what they would most like to emulate about him.

March 18

....

If one advances confidently in
the direction of his dreams, and endeavors
to live the life he imagined, he will
meet with a success unexpected
in common hours.

—Henry David Thoreau

March 19

•••

*I would never trust a man who didn't
cry, he wouldn't be human.*

—Norman Schwarzkopf

_____

_____

_____

_____

_____

_____

_____

_____

_____

_____

_____

_____

_____

_____

_____

_____

_____

_____

March 20

··

*Never look down on anybody unless
you're helping him up.*

—The Reverend Jesse Jackson

_____

_____

_____

_____

_____

_____

_____

_____

_____

_____

_____

_____

_____

_____

_____

_____

_____

_____

March 21

• •

*Forgiveness is the answer to
the child's dream of a miracle by which
what is broken is made whole again, what
is soiled is again made clean.*

—Dag Hammarskjold

March 22

....

*The person who does not make
a choice makes a choice.*

—Jewish proverb

March 23

....

I think I can, I know I can,
I think I can, I know I can!

—*The Little Engine That Could*

High expectations and the self-fulfilling prophecy. Robert Rosenberg's important work, *Pygmalion in the Classroom*, established firmly in the public mind the idea of the self-fulfilling prophecy. Treat people as though they will succeed and they are much more likely to succeed; treat them as potential failures and they will likely fail.

It is vital to know that it isn't the expectation alone that creates the effect. Because people have erroneously believed this, they have often blamed the victim, by being unsympathetic and quite judgmental about those who fail when the teacher had high expectations and high demands. High expectation works quite well when two other factors are present—the first and most important is high support. If we want someone to succeed and we behave toward them as though we know that they can and will succeed, we must accompany that with creating a structure of support so that it is, in fact, possible for them to learn what they need to learn. When we build in high support, the second factor comes into play: The student begins to believe in the possibility of his/her success, too.

- We are all teachers, at some time, to someone. At work you may have an employee or a co-worker who needs to learn a new skill. At home your child is doing homework and struggling without your help. Saying, "I know you can do it, I have faith in you," is a good thing, but can you accompany this with some kind of support that would help ensure the achievement? Write about this in your journal.

- Think of a time when you were learning a difficult skill. What support did you receive or would you have liked to receive that you think would have made a difference?

March 24

••

Charity sees the need, not the cause.

—German proverb

The Hebrew word *tzedakah*, which is usually translated as "charity," actually means something closer to "right-action." The idea is that one ought to do the thing that is right even if the other person might not "deserve" it. The right action is the right action regardless. A panhandler approaches with a sign saying, "Homeless and hungry. What can you spare?" Your companion says, "It's a scam." You, however, reach into your pocket and give some money to this person, saying to yourself, "The giver has the choice of how to act and how to be. The giver doesn't have to investigate whether or not the other person is truly deserving. It is the act of giving which ennobles. I choose to be a giver. Thank God I have something to give!"

- How does this scene affect you? Have you been pestered by panhandlers in some urban setting? How did you handle the decision to give or walk past?

- If the giver "makes a mistake" and gives something to a person who is unworthy, does it tarnish the act of giving?

- What needs do you see that need to be addressed in your neighborhood, your community or our country? Is there something you can do about them?

March 25

....

*Living well and beautifully and
justly are all one thing.*

—Sophocles

March 26

....

We must develop and maintain
the capacity to forgive. He who is devoid
of the power to forgive is devoid of the
power to love. There is some good in the
worst of us and some evil in the best of us.
When we discover this, we are less
prone to hate our enemies.

—The Reverend Martin Luther King Jr.

March 27

....

This is Daddy's bedtime secret for today:
Man is born broken. He lives by mending.
The grace of God is glue.

—Eugene O'Neill

March 28

....

> *Say I love you to those you love.
> The eternal silence is long enough to be
> silent in and that awaits us all.*

—George Eliot

_____

_____

_____

_____

_____

_____

_____

_____

_____

_____

_____

_____

_____

_____

_____

_____

_____

March 29

··

There is sublime thieving in all giving.
Someone gives us all he has
and we are his.

—Eric Hoffer

March 30

....

> *The mind ought sometimes to be
> diverted, that it may return
> the better to thinking.*
>
> —Phaedrus

Hobbies and pastimes are kindnesses to the self and to those with whom we live. Having interests beyond the mundane concerns of our jobs and housework bring joy, relief from stress, surcease of boredom and topics for conversation.

- When was the last time you took a break from your chores and tasks and just did something for the pure interest and enjoyment of it? Is it time for you to do that again now?

- Suggest to a friend or family member that you have an adventure. Plan it together. Set a theme for the day such as "Bridges" or "Below the Surface" or "Youth and Age." Bring along a camera. Jot down some ideas that occur to you at this very moment.

- How did your adventure go? Did it clear out the feeling of stuckness and sameness? Did you feel refreshed?

- Design a way to bring useful diversion into your life regularly. When are the moments you seem to need it most?

- Many Fortune 500 companies have discovered that such diversions during the workday can engender a considerable amount of creativity. Write some ideas about how you can bring this concept to your workplace.

March 31

....

*Remember, you show courtesy
to others not because they are gentlemen,
but because you are one.*

—Anonymous

Society is held together by the actions of civil gentlemen and gentlewomen. Being such a person takes great strength and courage in the face of adversity. It often means taking control of your emotions and rationally thinking beyond how you feel. Be a trend-setter; be a gentleperson.

- How would you define the term gentleman or gentlewoman?
- Who, historically, might fit this definition?
- Experiment today, and act as if you were this person, instead of merely reacting to others.

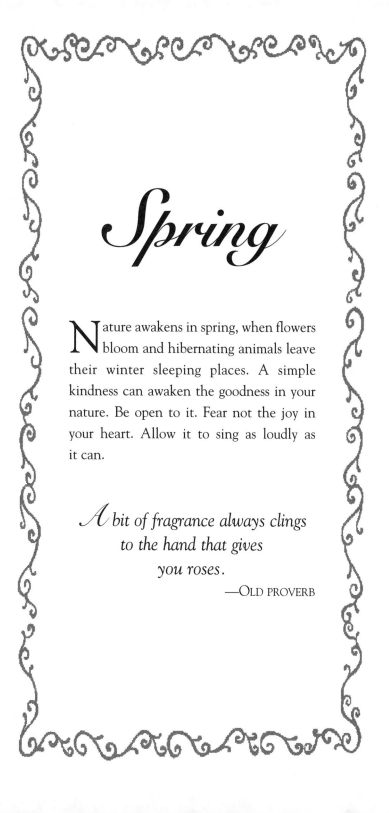

Spring

Nature awakens in spring, when flowers bloom and hibernating animals leave their winter sleeping places. A simple kindness can awaken the goodness in your nature. Be open to it. Fear not the joy in your heart. Allow it to sing as loudly as it can.

A bit of fragrance always clings to the hand that gives you roses.

—OLD PROVERB

April

Deliberate Acts of Kindness
for Passover and Easter

Thoughts:

Passover is one of the most important holidays on the Jewish religious calendar. It is a celebration of redemption from slavery and of thanksgiving. Traditionally, it is the time when families gather together to celebrate and to rejoice in each other and in their freedom. To understand this eight-day holiday you'd have to combine Thanksgiving with July 4th! Passover is celebrated at a dinner/prayer service called a *seder* at which everyone at the table participates, from the very youngest to the oldest. All have a role to play and the accent is on enjoyment and on the strengthening of family ties.

Easter, too, is one of the most important holidays on the Christian calendar. Although these two holidays are not always exactly simultaneous (because of the differences between the solar calendar the Western world uses and the lunar calendar employed by the Jewish faith), they once coincided, since the Last Supper was, in fact, a Passover seder! Easter is a celebration of renewal and spiritual rebirth. It symbolizes the gift of grace and the offer of redemption from God to mankind.

Both holidays are harbingers of spring, with all its hope of life and growth. Both offer opportunities for families to deepen their connections with each other.

Actions:

- Make sure that everyone is invited to this year's celebration. Do the peace-keeping and delicate negotiations to help smooth over ruffled feelings if distance has developed between certain family members.

- Both holidays have a traditional use of eggs to symbolize renewal. Get some hollow plastic eggs and put an affirmation for each family member in an egg to be opened at the dinner table.

- Ask everyone who's coming to bring their favorite recipe and then create a family cookbook to be distributed later.

- Invite a member of the armed services who is far from home during this holiday. Make a place during your Easter dinner or Passover seder for this person to share a little of his/her life, family traditions and feelings on this holiday.

- Build in ways for the children to participate in the preparations for this holiday celebration.

- Make a commitment—and ask for the same commitment from your family—to focus your energies on being kind, loving, caring and concerned for others during this holiday. Don't let the tumult of preparing for the holiday create so much stress that people begin snapping at each other. Let what you *do* be controlled by *how you want to be* so that everyone will *get* the closeness and love that are the hallmarks of these holy days.

April 1

....

*No one is useless in the world
who lightens the burden of it
for anyone else.*

—Charles Dickens

We would all like our lives to be meaningful and worthwhile. People get this sense of value in life from several sources—the belief in a higher power or in something outside the self that is bigger and more significant than we, and from service to others.

Of all the feedback that makes people feel good, the one that hits the bull's eye most frequently is when you are told that something you've done "made a difference" for someone else. "When you helped me with that project, I suddenly felt as though I could do it. I had given up before you offered to help. Thank you."

- Can you help someone feel useful and important by letting them help you in some way?

- Make a list of people who have been significantly helpful to you in your life recently. Ask yourself how you thanked them for their help. Is there anyone on your list who needs to be told of your gratitude?

April 2

....

*G*ive me a ready hand rather
than a ready tongue.

—Giuseppi Garibaldi

"All talk and no action" is a folk phrase that illustrates why some committees and people accomplish little. We think that you have a choice of parts to play in the game of life: an active player who leaps in and gets involved, a hand-wringer who moans "Ain't it awful?" a bench-sitter who misses the chance to play, a Monday morning quarterback who criticizes the choices of the other players or a referee who stays out of the game and merely judges. When the umpire cries, "Play ball!" which will you choose to be? Remember, though, that even the spectators get to cheer the players and help encourage them to go on.

- Have you ever been stuck in a situation with people who'd rather build mountains of words than anything real and concrete? How did you feel? How did you respond to the situation?

- One true act of kindness is to "do one's job with quiet competence." There's nothing flashy about this and such people may remain the unsung heroes who keep everything working and the process moving. But our society cannot work without them. Think of someone you know who is like that. Write a letter to this person acknowledging his or her contribution.

- Which of the roles described above is the one you usually play? Does it work for you? How would you change the way you play the game of life when it comes to acts of kindness?

- Do you ever shuttle from one role to another—a spectator at one time, an active player at another?
- Can you think of some gentle ways of encouraging others to take more action?

April 3

....

W*hen the heart is full,*
the eyes overflow.

—Sholem Aleichem

_____

_____

_____

_____

_____

_____

_____

_____

_____

_____

_____

_____

_____

_____

_____

_____

April 4

....

> *Live every day as if it were your last.*
> *Do every job as if you were the boss. Drive*
> *as if all other vehicles were police cars.*
> *Treat everybody else as if he were you.*
>
> —Anonymous

April 5

....

Do not do unto others as you
would that they should do unto you.
Their tastes may not be the same.

—George Bernard Shaw

April 6

··

> *T*here will always be a
> frontier where there is an open
> mind and a willing hand.
>
> —Charles F. Kettering

April 7

....

Ninety percent of all mental
illness that comes before me could have
been prevented, or cured, by
ordinary kindness.

—Dr. William McGrath

April 8

∙∙∙

*Make a rule, and pray to God
to help you to keep it, never, if possible, to
lie down at night without being able to say:
"I have made one human being at least
a little wiser, or a little happier, or
at least a little better this day."*

—Charles Kingsley

We can choose to make rules for ourselves, which though onerous, are at least self-imposed. If we chafe under their restrictions, it is at least not with rebellion against or resignation to other's dominance. Another option is to make guidelines or express intentions. A clear intention to be kind to others is productive without adding the dimension of guilt or self-condemnation when we fail to live up to a rule. Kindness probably ought to be a joyous thing, something we look forward to with delight rather than a drudgery we'd prefer to avoid.

April 9

....

W hen *a person is down in the world,*
an ounce of help is better than
a pound of preaching.

—Edward G. Bulwer-Lytton

"I told you so." There's often a delicious pleasure in
that phrase. "You goofed and I knew it would
happen. You've made a mistake and I am proved right
again." Those who utter these phrases are not endearing themselves to the one to whom they speak. It can
be so easy to speak to another from a morally superior
position. How much more loving it can be to swallow
those words and simply pitch in, and quietly help
repair the damage. The lesson is usually learned
without crude blows to the other person's sense of self.

- Think about the times when you've said, "I told
  you so," or something like it. Were they mostly
  said to people to whom you are very close? Why
  do you think that is so?

- Have you ever received a lecture when you just
  needed a hand? How did you feel then?

- If you could teach children (yours or anyone's)
  one thing about this, what would it be? Write
  down your thoughts and then decide who would
  benefit the most from your sharing them.

April 10

··

To the coronation of Edward the VII
notables from all over the world were
invited. One of the honored guests was the
Prime Minister of New Zealand, Alfred
Deakin. When he returned home he was
asked by reporters what was the most
impressive aspect of the coronation.
He answered by telling them of a sight he
saw one night as he passed a dark alley
in the poorest section of London. A little lad
of about 12 was sitting on a bleak doorstep
with his arm hugging a little girl about
half his age. The hour was late and the night
was cold and the little boy had draped his
frayed jacket around the little girl's
shoulders. His worn cap covered her bare
feet. And that, said Alfred Deakin, was the
sight that had left the deepest impression
on him at the coronation. So much in our
time has conspired to empty our lives
of meaning, to reduce them to mere
biological functions, serving no ultimate
purpose. Edna St. Vincent Millay expresses
the mood of our time in her weary words:
"Life must go on; I forget just why."
We have indeed lost the why of life.

—Sidney Greenberg, *Hidden Hungers*

April 11

....

*If we could not hope for a second
chance when life inflicts a severe defeat on
us, if we could not hope for strength
when we have been betrayed, if we could
not hope for wisdom when we are
confused, if we could not hope for healing
when we have been bruised, if we
could not hope for consolation when we
have been bereaved, if we could not hope
for eternity when the imminence of
winter drives home the inescapable fact of
our mortality, if in all these trials hope
should not well up within our breasts—
the burden of life would become
insufferable. Let us beware of those
who would rob us of our hopes.*

—Hartmore House

_____

_____

_____

_____

_____

_____

_____

_____

April 12

Kindness is the sunshine in which virtue grows.

—Robert G. Ingersoll

April 13

....

W*hat is unspoken is not
unexpressed. One morning when he
thought I was asleep, I heard my father
walk softly into the kitchen near my
room and begin slowly unloading the
dishwasher. I lay in bed, listening to how
gently he lifted out each pan, each glass.
Like the stealthiest thief in reverse,
he returned the silverware to its drawer.
He took 20 minutes to do what he could
have done in five, just to let me dream.
Once in a while, we are lucky enough
to be awake when love performs
in silent testaments.*

—Jenijoy La Belle

April 14

··

When you rise in the morning,
say that you will make the day blessed to a
fellow creature. It is easily done: a left-off
garment to the man who needs it; a kind
word to the sorrowful; an encouraging
expression to the struggling—trifles in
themselves as light as air will do at least for
the 24 hours. And if you are young,
depend upon it, it will tell when you are old;
and if you are old, rest assured
it will send you gently down the stream of
time to eternity. By the most simply
arithmetical sum, look into the result. If you
send one person away happy through the
day, there are 365 in the course of a year.
And suppose you live 40 years only.
After you commence that course of
medicine, you have made 14,600 persons
happy, at all events for a time.

—Anonymous

April 15

· ·

The race of mankind
would perish did they cease to aid
each other. We cannot exist without mutual
help. All therefore that need aid have a
right to ask it from their fellow-men; and no
one who has the power of granting
can refuse it without guilt.

—Sir Walter Scott

We seem to be tied up today in a struggle between the charitable feelings we have when we see someone in need and the undeniable problems created by so-called entitlement programs when we have third and fourth generation welfare families. The politics seem to cloud our ability to see that there are people hurting out there, children without food and families without housing.

- What's *your* take on this issue?

- Various programs tying welfare assistance to work or to attendance in drug rehabilitation have been proposed. Have you achieved any clarity about them? Write down your ideas. Discuss them, gently, with a friend.

- Is there a place in your community where you could suggest a kinder, gentler way of helping people gain skills and find jobs that would break the cycle of dependence on public assistance?

April 16

• •

*It is easier to be a critic
than a creator.*

—Anonymous

Recently, at a show, we met a man who offered us criticism about our last book. The very idea of a book about kindness seemed to offend him. He went on incessantly until his wife led him away, a pained and apologetic expression on her face. We thought about what it must be like to live with such a person. Carl Rogers, the great psychologist, told a story of being in the midst of conducting a seminar at a retreat center on a beautiful seashore. Suddenly, he said, a participant called out, "Look! A rainbow!" The whole group abandoned listening to Dr. Rogers and ran to the meeting room windows to enjoy the spectacle. Dr. Rogers too, went to see the rainbow. Standing next to him was one seminar student who was muttering, "Yeah, but it's not as good as the rainbow I saw last month." Dr. Rogers then remarked, "For some people out there, even *God* can get a mediocre grade! There are people who cannot let themselves fully enjoy or appreciate any experience."

• Are there things about which you are often a critic? What is on your critic list? Can you think of anyone you know who is annoyed by or hurt by your criticism?

• Do you interrupt someone who starts to tell a joke you've heard before? Do you moan and groan at someone's joke that you didn't appreciate? Do you roll your eyes and sigh exasperatedly when your spouse/friend/partner begins to tell a story you've heard "a hundred times?" Does this list suggest some acts of kindness you can perform by simply deciding to stop being a critic and start being an appreciator?

• Growth opportunity: How can you share this insight with the important people in your life?

April 17

••

My father is a happy man
not from trying to be, but because he
lives at the center. He understands how to
simplify the complexities of life. He does
something each day toward clearing his
own path through the wilderness, within
and without. There is at the core of
his being a mysterious strength I will never
fully comprehend, nor to which any
greeting card can speak.

—Jenijoy La Belle

April 18

··

I believe that every human mind feels
pleasure in doing good to another.

—Thomas Jefferson

April 19

....

> It is not so much consequence what you
> say, but how kindly you say it.
>
> —Ryan Joseph Bendell

April 20

···

S*trong is the soul, kind, and wise,*
and beautiful.

—Matthew Arnold

_____

_____

_____

_____

_____

_____

_____

_____

_____

_____

_____

_____

_____

_____

_____

_____

_____

April 21
....

*B*etter one deed than a thousand sighs.

—Rabbi Shalom Dou Ber of Lubavitch

April 22

....

*H*uman kindness has never
weakened the stamina or softened the
fiber of a free people. A nation does not
have to be cruel in order to be tough.

—Franklin Delano Roosevelt

America, for all its supposed toughness, is known around the world as one of the most charitable nations. We do give much toward charitable institutions and programs. When Hurricane Andrew hit Florida, people all over the country responded with donations of food, clothing, medical supplies, tools, building equipment. Many people flew in, at their own expense, and helped. Two years later, when the Mississippi River flooded so many towns, the people of South Florida filled many freight cars with their donations. We seem to be a country that knows how to respond to disaster.

- We've been told repeatedly that "kindness is for wimps." Do these acts by ordinary citizens, by electricians and carpenters and plumbers and farmers, sound wimpy to you? Why is it that some people seem cynical about kindness but seem ready to leap into action to help when others are hurting?

- Consider the phrase, "Kindness takes courage." Think about how it has been true in your life.

- Our choices of how to act and what to say are powerful models for our children and our peers. How shall we talk about kindness to help others make sense of it?

- Pretend you were going to write a letter to the editor of your local newspaper about the place kindness holds in our society. What would you say? Okay, now write it and mail it. Our country needs you to stand up and be counted.

April 23

....

*N*egative energy seems,
in many people, to be eight times
stronger than positive energy.

—Hanoch McCarty

Many large corporations and department stores report that they receive about eight times as many letters of complaint as they do letters of commendation. Why is that? We seem to be motivated to take action more when we're annoyed than when we are delighted. The clerk who ignores you stimulates anger; the clerk who serves you well is merely doing what he or she is supposed to do, therefore, grateful as we may be, we go on with our business without thinking to write appreciatively to the company.

You pass your child's room and notice an awful mess. Your disappointment is immediately expressed, sometimes angrily. If it should ever be neat and clean, you may forget to say anything, since that's how the room should be anyway.

These examples illustrate why our criticisms may be more evident to others than our kindness.

- Are you "quick to anger, slow to praise"? Is this how you want to be? Does it work for you?

- Some people like to see themselves as out of control. "I just couldn't help myself, it just came out of me, I *had* to yell at him." Do you see yourself as able to decide not to criticize? Are you capable of reversing the "eight-to-one" ratio and give out more affirmations than criticisms to the important people in your life?

- What would be the impact on your home life and your work life if you successfully altered the ratio of negatives to positives in the feedback you give to others?

April 24

....

*There's only one corner of the
universe you can be certain of improving
and that's your own self.*

—Aldous Huxley

April 25
....

Have patience with all things,
but chiefly have patience with yourself.
Do not lose courage in considering
your own imperfections, but instantly set
about remedying them. Every day
begin the task anew.

—Francis De Sales

_____

_____

_____

_____

_____

_____

_____

_____

_____

_____

_____

_____

_____

April 26

··

When love and skill work together,
        expect a masterpiece.

—John Ruskin

_____

_____

_____

_____

_____

_____

_____

_____

_____

_____

_____

_____

_____

_____

_____

_____

_____

April 27

A heart that lives in grace.

—Dante Alighieri

....

Sorrow shared is halved and joy
shared is doubled.

—Native American saying

_____

_____

_____

_____

_____

_____

_____

_____

_____

_____

_____

_____

_____

_____

_____

_____

April 29

···

*The unfortunate need people
who will be kind to them; the prosperous
need people to be kind to.*

—Aristotle

Life is given its meaning by our interactions with others. These special, sometimes ordinary moments, are what give our lives texture and depth.

When we are weary and down on our luck, we benefit from the kindness of others until we can get back on our feet. Once we have reached a state of emotional and/or material prosperity, we can most benefit from assisting others. This is what gives our lives meaning.

- In what ways do you consider yourself prosperous?

- Are there others that you know who are less fortunate than you in this regard? How might you help them?

April 30

....

For it is in giving that we receive.

—St. Francis of Assisi

We should give to others merely for the joy in making someone's day, seeing them smile or cry tears of happiness. Giving does not necessarily mean a gift of money. Giving of your time is just as important.

- List five things you can give to others today. Be specific about what you will give and to whom you will give it.

- Make a contract with yourself promising to do at least one of these kind acts of giving next week. Sign and date the document. Give it to someone who will hold you to your promise.

May

Deliberate Acts of Kindness for Mother's Day
(Second Sunday in May)

As authors of *Acts of Kindness: How to Create a Kindness Revolution*, we've traveled all over the country talking with people who practice kindness in a variety of ways. Most often people will comment about the kind actions of their mother or mother figure. They will mention values their mother taught them or support she gave to them in troubled times. Meladee's mother, Laura Spiess, has spent many years in a wheelchair because of multiple sclerosis and yet she has never complained or focused on her troubles. Instead, she greets the world each day with the sunniest of smiles and always asks how *you* are. She celebrates others unfailingly and demonstrates the highest integrity and love. Hanoch's mother, Jean McCarty, was warm, witty and wise. She was the most entertaining hostess, the funniest story-teller, the most fascinating and intelligent problem-solver. Each of our parents taught us powerful lessons about living with high integrity and about how to be loving in a world that might, at times, seem cold.

We've put a few ideas together for you to think about as Mother's Day approaches. Remember what Mom said, "It's the thought that counts!" Great gifts for Mother's Day don't have to cost a lot of money—instead they should simply be evidence of your having spent time, love, attention, thoughtfulness. This is a chance to celebrate and repay Mom just a little bit for all that she has given.

- Fill an attractive jar with encouraging messages, quotes, and special thank-you's for the things your mother did for you. Make enough for her to read every day for one month. This is something she'll look forward to on a daily basis, long after the excitement of Mother's Day.

- Just for today, decide that you will respond without anger to events that usually make you mad. Decide to be a forgiving person, just for today. When Mom told you to "count to ten" before expressing anger, she was right: Studies show that pausing like that can break the anger cycle and allow you to be more in control of your reactions. Give Mom the gift of showing that you really can learn to live her lessons of forgiveness, patience and caring.

- Name garden: Place potting soil in a large foil pan. Plant sprouts, or tiny flower seeds, to spell Mom's name. Be sure to begin this project a couple of weeks before Mother's Day.

- Treasure hunt: Hide love messages throughout your mom's house. Put them in her shoes, by the phone, sachet bag, bathtub and silverware drawer, and put her favorite ice cream in the freezer. It's fun to put funny pictures along with the notes.

- Create new words to an old song, with her name and special qualities in the lyrics.

- Make a plaque for her wall with her photo, celebrating the values she has taught and modeled for you—honesty, hope, courage, kindness, support, etc.)

- Before it's inflated, slip a message into a helium balloon, saying something like, "You're one in a million Mom. Your presence in my life fills me with joy, and constantly lifts my spirits."

- Send Mother's Day wishes from famous people. "Let me be the first to wish you happy Mother's Day, it is mothers like you that make this nation great," from Bill Clinton. "I love you, you love me, we're a happy family, with a great big hug and a kiss from me to you, Happy Mother's Day to you," from Barney. "There should be a monument built in your honor," from Lincoln. "Make my day. Have a happy Mother's Day," from Clint Eastwood.

- Hire someone from your local high school or college music department to serenade her with a song of love from you.

- Send your mother a Mother's Day card for every year she's been your mother.

- Coupons are always fun and affordable. Some examples: "Let me wash the dishes for you for a week, to give your hard-working hands a rest." "Good for one car wash so that you can drive in style." "Good for the service of your choice, performed with a good attitude."

- Take continuous-feed computer paper with "Mom" written at the top. Under her name, write, "We love you more than all the chocolate in the candy store, more than all the fish in the sea and birds in the sky." Leave a box of felt pens nearby so that other family members can contribute to the banner.

- Take Mom on a picnic. Don't forget the flowers, candles and music.

- Start a Mother's Day club. Some mothers won't have their families with them for the holiday or will have lost their children and have no one to celebrate them. Get a bunch of Mother's Day cards and send them out to other mothers that need to be celebrated, too.

- Make a tape of your mom's favorite songs and add a special message reminding her why she's so important to you.

- Give Mom a massage. As you rub her tired shoulders, thank her for all the troubles she's shouldered throughout the years. Rubbing her temples, thank her for all the times she helped you think through problems or challenges you faced. Gently massage her hands and appreciate her for all the TLC she dishes out to comfort you. Rub her arms and thank her for the hugs that sheltered you from harm. Knead her back and celebrate her for having a strong back-bone, standing up for her values and not giving up what she believes in.

- Make an acronym out of Mom's name.
  For example Carrie:
  C: caring, clever, confident, conscientious, courteous, creative, cute, cuddly, courageous, capable, calming, comforting, compliment-ing, considerate, cooperative, competent, consistent.
  A: artistic, attractive, accepting, advising, acknowledging, adorable, affirming, awesome.
  R: realistic, receptive, reciprocal, respectful, responsible.
  R: rare, radiating, refreshing, resplendent, real.
  I: independent, interesting, intellectual, ideal, imaginative, impartial, impeccable.
  E: endearing, exciting, encouraging, earnest, easygoing, effectual, efficient, embracing, engaging, enthusiastic, essential, exemplary.

- Make a humor kit for Mom to help her when she's stuck in traffic or in a doctor's waiting room. This helps lower her stress level and get past tough situations in a relaxed and playful manner. Things to include in a kit might be a red clown nose, Groucho glasses, bubbles and bubble blower, confetti, and horn.

- Donate funds to a homeless women's shelter in her name.

- Purchase a diary for Mom. Bookstores carry some with blank pages. Title this diary, "Mom's Thankful Book." In it list all the things about her that you are thankful for. This can be a valuable support to her when times get tough and her spirits are low.

- Plant trees in Mom's community park in her name.

- Donate a bouquet of flowers in her name to her place of worship.

- Take Mom on a trip called, "Mom's Memory Lane." Do a little research around the year you were born and if you have siblings, research the years they were born. Type the highlights and include a note that says, "The world has changed quite a lot since I was born, but the best things in life remain the same. I still have the world's best mom."

- Do Mom's spring cleaning for her while you send her and a friend out to lunch.

- Consider Mom's point of view. Don't discuss religion or politics with her. Laugh at her jokes. Listen to her without interrupting. Say, "I love you," often, not just on Mother's Day.

- Bring Mom a beautiful plant, but rename it in her honor—Beautiful Betty, Lovely Laura, Sweet Sarah. Don't forget a name-tag for the plant and care instructions.

- If your mom has passed away, celebrate her memory with a donation to a local library or to a day-care center or pre-school program. One thing that you can donate is your time as a volunteer. Another thing you can do is donate money to establish a shelf of books on good parenting, which they can lend to parents of children at their center. Name that shelf in your mom's memory.

Deliberate Acts of Kindness
for Memorial Day:
(Last Monday in May)

Thoughts:

Memorial Day began as Decoration Day, an event to commemorate all those who died in America's Civil War and the Spanish American War. It widened to include the deceased from the First World War. We have since had many conflicts and many people have given their lives in the struggles to defend our country and its liberty.

Consider your own feelings about liberty, about patriotism, about sacrifice and about war. Is a holiday such as this a meaningful one for you? How has it affected your life?

- Has a member of your own family died in war? Think about their sacrifice and the impact it still has on you and your family.

- Did you serve in the military? In time of war? If so, what feelings or ideas are stimulated in you at this time of year? Was your service a conscious choice or fate?

- What debt does America owe to its war dead and to its veterans? What small part of that debt do you choose to take on?

Actions:

- Gather some friends and neighbors and organize an *oral history project* in your town. Record on tape interviews with veterans and with their spouses. Interview survivors of soldiers who died in foreign wars. Involve your local veterans' associations—American Legion, Veterans of Foreign

Wars, etc.—as well as local high school or middle school students to help with this project. Have the results stored in the school's library or the local public library.

- Celebrate Memorial Day by going to a parade or attending a ceremony, or by visiting your local cemetery. Volunteer to decorate some gravestones with flags or bunting. *Decide that today is not just an excuse for another sale at the mall.* Teach your children about what the day means and why we celebrate it. Make it personal.

- Have a conversation with someone you know who is a veteran or a close family member of a veteran. Ask them to tell you their story. What did their war mean to them? What sacrifices did they have to make? Be the best listener that you can be.

- Contact some of the senior citizen volunteer groups in your community. Ask if they are planning anything special for Memorial Day. If so, get involved. If not, suggest that they plan something and offer your services as a volunteer. Get other *recruits* involved.

- Contact an editor at your local paper and suggest that a small group of local soldiers who died in America's wars be commemorated in a special article each Memorial Day. Perhaps the article could include photographs of them from childhood until they entered the service, stories about them written by their families, etc.

May 1

· ·

As one whom his mother comforteth,
so will I comfort you.

—Old Testament Isa. 66:13

Good parents give us nurturing, unconditional love, firm direction, unlimited support. When faced with setbacks, failures, losses, we learn that we can count on our parents for the sustaining comfort that allows us to rebuild ourselves and confront our challenges once more. "It takes a whole community to raise a child." Today is your time to add your strong hand to comfort someone.

- Our parents or other caring adults taught us nurturing skills by their example. What kindnesses did you learn as a child?

- How have you used these nurturing examples in your life?

- Who do you know, right now, that could really use some nurturing care? How could you offer it to them?

- Sometimes, we need to transcend the caring we received as children. Perhaps our own experience was not as nurturing as we needed. Are there any ways in which you've learned to go beyond your own childhood models?

- Today you can express caring to one person, or you could volunteer to work in a child-care center, or you could donate time or materials to a center for homeless children. The possibilities are endless.

May 2
....

Charity *begins at home.*

—Terence

You *always hurt the one you love.*

—Oscar Wilde

There are people who find it much easier to be consistently kind to strangers and co-workers rather than to their families. The closeness breeds a kind of taking for granted and a disregard of the others' feelings—perhaps because we have so many agendas, hopes and wishes for our family members.

- How does your family see you in the area of kindness? Do they see you as kind to all equally or as less energetic in your reaching out to those at home? How was it for you in your childhood home?

- Do you repeat patterns similar to those you saw as a child? In what ways do you differ?

- Think about the balance in your life between the kindnesses, energy and attention you give inside and outside of your family. Write about this balance and your conclusions.

- In what ways is your family bringing charity to the world? Do you have a sense of "family mission"? What might it be? Ask your family to help define this and plan ways to take action on it.

May 3

....

One word frees us of all the weight and
pain of life: That word is love.

—Sophocles

May 4
....

One loves a specific person or
is his friend not because he belongs to the
same nation, the same party or the
same religion as oneself but, sometimes in
spite of all that, simply because
he is what he is.

—Ignace Lepp

_____

_____

_____

_____

_____

_____

_____

_____

_____

_____

_____

_____

_____

_____

May 5

When we surrender to love,
we lose our self-centeredness and surge
toward those we love.

—Richard Henry Stoddard

May 6

· ·

*J*oy is an achievement;
it presupposes an inner effort: that of
productive activity.

—Erich Fromm

May 7

....

A̶ll thoughts, all passions,
all delights, whatever stirs this mortal
frame, all are but ministers of love,
and feed his sacred flame.

—Samuel Taylor Coleridge

May 8

The best portion of a good man's life is his little, nameless, unremembered acts of kindness and of love.

—William Wordsworth

Some kindnesses are so unremarkable that one almost never acknowledges them out loud. My mother couldn't go to the refrigerator without coming back with a cold drink for everyone else watching TV. My brother Douglas would automatically restrain me when he suddenly stopped his car—even though I was wearing a seatbelt. My son called me one morning from college just because I was on his mind as he awoke. People would quietly run ahead to open doors for Meladee's mom, who used a walker. These acts, unremarkable in themselves, bring comfort and reassurance. When all is said and done, they may be our greatest legacy.

- Make an extensive list of the little kindnesses you've received from someone important to you. Take as much time as you need.

- Did you find that this task resulted in pleasant reminiscences and sweet conversations with others? What effect do those memories have on you?

- Now make a list of your little kindnesses that might be written by those who know you. How do you feel about that list? Does making *this* list make you want to change your own behavior in any way?

- What little kindnesses would you like to add to your repertoire? How do you think you can begin?

May 9

....

If you want to criticize,
you must first create a context for
criticism, or your relationship will be
damaged and the criticism will
not accomplish its purpose.

—Hanoch McCarty

Think of relationships as social bank accounts, with each person having an account in the other's "bank." Each time I am with the other person, we transact the business of the account. If I spend time with you, that is at least a small deposit in your account. If I compliment you, give you attention, or hug you, each of these acts makes a deposit of a certain value into your account. And you do the same with my account, too. When I ignore you, am too busy to spend time with you, and especially when I criticize you, I am making withdrawals from your account. In our heart of hearts, we have a "teller" who is continually monitoring the balance in each of our accounts, letting us know how well we are doing with friends, family and co-workers.

Exploring this metaphor further, it is a dangerous practice to make withdrawals from accounts into which I have made few or no deposits. I can quickly become overdrawn and have my account closed, my checks ignored or refused.

Just as effort is required to keep your accounts in balance, especially those with a large positive balance, relationships, too, take that kind of work and thought. We are not suggesting that you never criticize. Indeed, there are times when it is necessary. It may be required by your situation. However, your criticisms do have to come in a context of a healthy relationship, one that has been nurtured and strengthened by positive affirmations and time spent with those who are important to you. Having put in the time, shared skills and knowledge, any criticism you make is more likely to be seen as valid *and survivable* if it is just one part of a more rounded and complete relationship.

- How do you think the important people in your life see you in regard to criticism and negativity?

- Think of three to five people in your life who are most important to you for whatever reasons (parents, children, friends, neighbors, colleagues, spouse). Have you given them a healthy context for your relationship?

- An effective affirmation should be real, authentic, representing your genuine feelings. It should be short and specific. Long or vague affirmations can raise confusion or suspicion. Finally, if you affirm regularly rather than rarely, the relationship is strengthened.

May 10

....

T*hat is the happiest conversation*
where there is no competition, no vanity,
but a calm, quiet interchange
of sentiments.

—Samuel Johnson

_____

_____

_____

_____

_____

_____

_____

_____

_____

_____

_____

_____

_____

_____

_____

_____

May 11
....

> *H*old *faithfulness and sincerity*
> *as first principles.*
>
> —Confucius

_____

_____

_____

_____

_____

_____

_____

_____

_____

_____

_____

_____

_____

_____

_____

_____

_____

_____

May 12

....

Life is an opportunity, benefit from it.
Life is a beauty, admire it.
Life is bliss, taste it.
Life is a dream, realize it.
Life is a challenge, meet it.
Life is a duty, complete it.
Life is a game, play it.
Life is costly, care for it.
Life is wealth, keep it.
Life is love, enjoy it.
Life is mystery, know it.
Life is a promise, fulfill it.
Life is sorrow, overcome it.
Life is a song, sing it.
Life is a struggle, accept it.
Life is a tragedy, confront it.
Life is an adventure, dare it.
Life is luck, make it.
Life is too precious, do not destroy it.
Life is life, fight for it!

—Mother Teresa

_____

_____

_____

_____

May 13

....

Love everybody you love; you can never
tell when they might not be there.

—Nancy Bush Ellis

_____

_____

_____

_____

_____

_____

_____

_____

_____

_____

_____

_____

_____

_____

_____

_____

_____

May 14

. . . .

*K*indness . . . *loving people more
than they deserve.*

—Joseph Joubert

May 15

....

> Kindness is a language the wordless
> can speak and the deaf can
> hear and understand.
>
> —Christian Nestell Bovee

Communication is a tricky business. We've learned long ago that the message sent is not necessarily the message received. Communication experts talk about "encoding" one's thoughts into language and the listener "decoding" them. And in those two processes there are so many opportunities for misunderstanding. You may do a kindness and have it misperceived, the other person's past may get in the way and prevent your act from being understood. But, if you are patient and if your kindness is not occasional or accidental but constant and deliberate, you will communicate most eloquently.

- How has kindness communicated in your life? Can you think of moments when a kindness "spoke volumes"? Write some of these experiences in your journal.

- Cynics quote Mark Twain's sarcastic dictum: "No good deed goes unpunished." Has this been a part of your experience, too?

- Optimists retort with a quote from William Purkey: "No act of kindness is ever wasted." We experience kindness and caring as having a ripple effect and influencing many people and events that you may not see. How do you react to this idea?

May 16

....

*If you want to moan, complain,
or focus on your problems, it's okay with
me. But I have a two-for-one rule:
For every minute we spend on complaints,
we have to spend two on solutions to the
problem. If I have a half hour to spend
with you, 10 can be spent listening
to your problems and then you've got to
promise to spend 20 on figuring
out what to do about them.*

—Margie Ingram

It's amazing how quickly conversations can degenerate into "pity-parties." Victimhood has some powerful rewards, like attention, sympathy, and permission to remain stuck in the problem without ever having to take any action to change. In the Middle Ages, martyrs suffered, too, but had the courtesy to do so in silence! In our modern age, people seem to really enjoy trotting out their pains and problems and polishing them publicly, like treasured museum pieces.

Is it a kindness to provide an endless audience for these sad stories? We think it's a judgment call. It's important to have sympathy and TLC for someone, stunned by recent reverses, needing support. If, however, you sense that this is a well-rehearsed story or you know the person and have heard this tale repeatedly, wouldn't Margie Ingram's two-for-one rule make more sense? Wouldn't it be a great kindness for you to have the courage to insist, gently, that the person work on moving past the problem to some solution? And your second act of kindness would be to serve as sounding board and facilitator of the process.

- Are there any areas in your own life in which you think you've been stuck in a cycle of victimhood or inaction?

- Which people in your life come to mind when you think about this behavior of complaining and playing victim? Is it possible to confront them, lovingly, with the two-for-one rule?

- How would that affect your relationship with them? Are you willing to take the risk?

....

*L*ife teaches us to be less harsh with
ourselves and with others.

—Lin Yutang

May 18

Cultivate peace and harmony with all.

—George Washington

_____

_____

_____

_____

_____

_____

_____

_____

_____

_____

_____

_____

_____

_____

_____

_____

_____

May 19

···

All are needed by each one:
Nothing is fair or good alone.

—Ralph Waldo Emerson

May 20

....

> There is but one unconditional
> commandment . . . to bring about the
> very largest total universe of good
> which we can see.
>
> —William James

_____

_____

_____

_____

_____

_____

_____

_____

_____

_____

_____

_____

_____

_____

_____

_____

_____

_____

May 21

....

Be of good cheer.

—Homer

_____

_____

_____

_____

_____

_____

_____

_____

_____

_____

_____

_____

_____

_____

_____

_____

May 22

....

*Every year about a million
Americans give one or more pints of
blood to benefit people they've never met.
Nearly half of all American adults do
some kind of volunteer work.
People in seven out of 10 American
households contribute to charities.*

—M. Hunt, *The Compassionate Beast*

Every day thousands of people do absolutely spectacular acts of kindness. Most of the time they will not be featured on the front page of the newspaper. If you take the time to read the paper all the way through and highlight articles containing acts of kindness, you'll be surprised and encouraged to find many. We humans are far more caring than we've learned to expect.

- Ask a friend, a co-worker, a neighbor about their volunteer work. Or about someone they've helped recently. Conduct your own poll. See what you find out about the humans with whom you share the planet.

- Call your local church, synagogue or mosque. Ask to speak to the clergyperson and ask those same questions. Ask about volunteers and programs for them. Continue your private poll. Write the results in your journal.

- Have you been surprised about good things that are done, the good deeds people do with little or no fanfare? Do you think that it would be important or useful to share this knowledge? With whom? Plan a way to share your information with children, co-workers or even with the media in your town. Do you think it could help change the way in which your community is seen by its citizens?

May 23

....

*T*here *oughta be a law!*

—Everybody

Gunnar Myrdal, the famous Swedish sociologist and author, visited America in the '30s and '40s and noted that Americans seemed always to want a law to be passed to solve some social problem, but simultaneously wanted the law to apply to everyone else except them! A good example is found on the highways. Everyone criticizes that speeding car whizzing by, but almost everyone speeds when they drive. And just who is it who buys all those radar detectors?

We watch the news and some daily tragedy or atrocity evokes a strong, almost visceral, response. We are horrified and concerned. "Someone ought to do something about that." If a politician responds with a suggestion, he or she is usually met with an instant storm of criticism.

Wouldn't it be a kindness if you decided on three modes of behavior the next time you see some problem that needs solving? 1. Instead of hoping someone else will do something, volunteer yourself. Do it now. Make that call. 2. If you're not willing to take action, refrain from criticizing those who do. 3. If you cannot or will not get involved personally, can you at least lend support to those who do? Send a donation. Send a letter of commendation. Write a letter of recognition to the editor.

- Watch tonight's six o'clock news. Ask yourself if there's a wrong that needs righting. Tune in to your own responses to the news.

- Listen for "there oughta be a law" kind of thinking. Are you guilty of it, too? Can you replace it with the three modes of behavior?

- What would happen in your community if you could spread this idea and recruit others to agree to it?

May 24
....

Live your life in a manner that never infringes on the happiness of anyone.

—Eknath Easwaran

_____

_____

_____

_____

_____

_____

_____

_____

_____

_____

_____

_____

_____

_____

_____

_____

_____

_____

May 25

··

*T*ake the gentle path.

—George Herbert

May 26

· ·

Live is exactly as strong as life.

—Joseph Campbell

_____

_____

_____

_____

_____

_____

_____

_____

_____

_____

_____

_____

_____

_____

_____

_____

_____

_____

May 27

....

*The joy of life is to put out
one's power in some natural and
useful or harmless way.*

—Oliver Wendell Holmes

_____

_____

_____

_____

_____

_____

_____

_____

_____

_____

_____

_____

_____

_____

_____

_____

_____

May 28

. . . .

Most people I meet are kind
or really want to be kind. I think that the
ever-increasing need to hustle just to make
a living has caused people to run scared,
to see themselves as not having time
for those things which used to bring grace
into one's life. So they look for quick
fixes and magic solutions—
"Is there a preprinted greeting card for
that occasion? I'll send it instead of taking
the time to make the call." And yet,
when reminded of the kinder alternative,
they sigh, smile and say, "Yes, I think
that's what I really need to do."

—Hanoch McCarty

May 29

∙∙

To fall down, you manage alone, but it takes friendly hands to get up.

—Carolee Dunagan

When we suffer a setback, we usually feel very alone. We can all relate at least one experience—being fired or laid off from a job, learning of a serious medical condition, being spurned by a love interest—where we bottomed out emotionally and felt as if the entire world were washing down around us. Yet if we step back from the situation and talk to others, we often find many other people who have been through a similar experience.

Having a support system of caring friends, family members and even kind strangers, can lift someone out of depression to a healing place.

Be a kind listener to someone who needs help. Even if you don't feel you have the right words, anything you say that comes from a place of love and thoughtfulness will be a much-needed boost to a person in need.

- Do you know someone who has recently suffered a trauma or setback? Be a kind friend and give him or her a call or send a friendly card.
- Start a collection of uplifting quotes in your journal. You can refer to them when you need them.

May 30

• •

*The whole worth of a kind deed lies in the
love that inspires it.*

—*The Talmud*

It is not the money we spend on gifts that matters, it is the thought that counts. A dozen dandelions are more precious than a dozen red roses if they are sent with genuine love in mind. The same can be said for kind deeds. Do them because you are inspired by love and goodness, not because you expect anything in return.

- Make a list of your dearest friends and loved ones. Write down the attributes that make them so special to you.
- What kind deeds could you do especially for these people?

May 31

....

*L*et us be kinder to one another.

—Aldous Huxley's last words

_____

_____

_____

_____

_____

_____

_____

_____

_____

_____

_____

_____

_____

_____

_____

_____

_____

June

Deliberate Acts of Kindness
for Father's Day
(Third Sunday in June)

As Father's Day approaches, it is good to think about your father and how much he means to you in your life. You may feel that you can never repay him for all the good and caring things he's done for you, but this is his day and this is your chance to at least make a down payment!

Here is a useful list of ideas, based on our best-selling book *Acts of Kindness: How to Create a Kindness Revolution*, which you can put into action right away to make this Father's Day a special and memorable one for your dad.

- If your dad is the kind of guy who always took the pictures of your family, make sure this year to take pictures that include him, prominently at the center of the action, rather than hidden behind the camera.

- Get a tape recorder ready and interview your dad about his life. He may be reticent and it may take several sessions to begin to get something usable, but persistence is the key to success. Ask him about his childhood, his dreams, hopes and plans. Ask him about his parents, his family and his friends. This will be fun to play on Father's Day now, and in years to come when he's no longer with you, the next generation may find this a gold mine of family lore.

- Listen to Dad. Really listen. Ask him about the stories that he loves to tell. You know, the stories you may have heard so often that you sigh and roll your eyes when he launches one of them? This time, listen without the attitude. Pay him some attention. Now resolve to do this regularly and not just on Father's Day.

- Make a donation to his favorite club or charity in his name. Set up something special for him. Example: a special bookshelf of good books on parenting at a local pre-school, day nursery or other agency and have the shelf called, "The (your father's name) Bookshelf for Fathers and Other Great People."

- If he's a gardener, plant the garden for him this year, under his supervision and following his plans. Make it as delightful and positive an experience as you can.

- Ask his advice about something he's good at. Or ask him to help fix something you know he's skilled at fixing. Many times, as kids grow up, their parents may begin to feel less and less useful or needed. Help Dad remember how needed he is and always has been.

- Make Father's Day as big a celebration in your family as Mother's Day. Help Dad feel valued and important and, especially, loved.

- Whatever Dad's hobby or pastime is, make plans to participate in it with him, at least for one day this month. Ask him to show you his collection or go with him to the ballpark.

- Thank him, in writing, for being there for you when there were many fathers in the world who didn't fulfill their parental obligations.

- Forgive Dad. Maybe he wasn't perfect or the *"Father Knows Best"* kind of father you wished for, but with all his imperfections, remember that he was doing the best that he knew how to do. There will come a day when you'll wish your children will forgive you for the gap between the ideal and the real parent you became.

- Organize a family reunion in his honor and be the peace-maker if there's a need to mend fences in the family. Make sure that everyone of importance to him is there. Remind them that "today is a gift and tomorrow is only a promise." You don't know how many more Father's Days you'll have him around—treasure him while you have him.

- Call his friends and ask them to tell you his special qualities as they see them. Write a list and give it to him—along with your own positive comments—in a decorated looseleaf book called, *Our Tribute to Dad*. Put in photographs of key moments in your lives.

- Tell Dad that you'll stick by him just as he has stuck by you. Loyalty is everything to fathers, you know.

- Take him fishing, to a ball game, on a hike or on a camping trip. Don't come home early.

- Have a serious conversation with your dad in which you tell him the values that you learned from him. Let him know that his lessons weren't wasted on you.

- Brag about your father in a place where he can overhear you. If you're giving a speech, conducting a program, writing a report, dedicate it to him and send him a copy. Or send him a copy of something you've done and write on it, "I could never have done this without all the things I learned from you, Dad."

- Send your father flowers. Mom liked hers, he'll like getting some, too.

June 1

••

*The greatest disease of mankind
is the absence of love.*

—Mother Teresa

My father used to tell me that my cleverness was a great strength for me, but also a source of potential undoing. "Don't let your cleverness get away with you," he'd say. As a teen, I did not understand. Today, as I watch what clever people have decided will appear on the six o'clock news, I understand what he meant. Their focus on the negative, choosing to ignore so much good that occurs each day, is their undoing and perhaps the undoing of us all. For they choose to see the world with their *minds* only, instead of with their *hearts* as well. Cleverly they ferret out crime, poverty, scandal, maleficence. Yet they walk past heroism, tenderness, self-sacrifice and the free offer of many loving hearts.

- What people in your life, past or present, have been or are your heroes of love and tenderness?

- What were the qualities they possessed that you have so admired?

- What are your similar qualities? How can you add to them?

- Each of us is a teacher for somebody. For whom might you become the model?

June 2

∙∙

It is a duty to cultivate kindness.

—Aaron Halevi, *Sefer Hallinuk*, c.1300

Some people think of prayer as separate from action. We think that your actions often constitute a prayer. The old saying, "God helps those who help themselves," illustrates how your response to a problem can stimulate more responses by others. Instead of waiting for divine intervention, you take action. Perhaps your action is, in fact, the way that God chose to intervene in the world today. If you see cruelty in the world, what will be your response? Will you bemoan it or take action to bring more kindness alive?

• Think of a situation that created a strong feeling in you, yet your response was delayed. You walk away and later think, "Why didn't I do something?" Write some of these in your journal.

• What action would you have taken if you could have done just the right thing?

• Which of your actions do you think could be considered your "prayers" today? Think about this today and make a decision about actions tomorrow.

....

No duty is more urgent than
that of returning thanks.

—St. Ambrose

June 4

··

*The more he gives to others, the more
he possesses of his own.*

—Lao-Tzu

_____

_____

_____

_____

_____

_____

_____

_____

_____

_____

_____

_____

_____

_____

_____

_____

_____

June 5

*T*he way to happiness—keep your heart
free from hate, your mind from worry, live
simply, expect little, give much.

—Carol Borges

June 6

....

*U*se no hurtful deceit;
think innocently and justly and, if you
speak, speak accordingly.

—Benjamin Franklin

_____

_____

_____

_____

_____

_____

_____

_____

_____

_____

_____

_____

_____

_____

_____

_____

_____

June 7

....

*The bravest are the tenderest,
the loving are the daring.*

—Bayard Taylor

June 8

W hat I hated most,
as a kid, was not being taken seriously.
Everything I said was "cute." How would
you like to be called cute all the time?
"You're cute when you're angry"
is a statement guaranteed to get a husband
in deep trouble. But everyone treats
kids as though they are
not quite real.

—Adrienne Wiesel

Children and people in wheelchairs are often treated this way. The waiter ignores the person in the wheelchair and asks someone else at the table, "What does he want to eat?" The parents discuss one of their children, in front of that child, as though the child were not there. Several teachers we know told us that in their first year of teaching, colleagues would sometimes discuss them, in front of them, in that same way. "Wait until she is here a few years, she'll wise up. Right now, she's still wet behind the ears." They reported that they were embarrassed and infuriated by this treatment.

- This is a treatment we don't give to people we fully respect. You cannot imagine behaving this way toward your employer, can you? So the issue comes down to one of respect. Whom do you respect? Is respect properly given to those much younger than you or junior in seniority to you? What do we mean by *respect*?

- Respect can be defined as treating the other person as someone of worth equal to yours. This does not mean pretending that they know as much as you do or are equally capable. As an adult, you certainly know much more about some things than most children. But can you treat each child as though he or she is of equal worth?

June 9

Blessed *is the man whose heart has no malice.*

—Apocrypha: 2 Bar., 44.4

It would be a wonderful and remarkable experience to meet a person with no malice in his heart. We think that most of us are probably flawed with feelings and thoughts we later wish we didn't have. Martin Buber said that to understand the human race, you have to accept that there are angels and devils, both, inside us. The most important thing about kindness is to make the decision to go on anyway, despite the flaws. Kindness doesn't require perfection, just good intent. Take that good intent, accept the rest of yourself as merely and beautifully human, and take kind action.

- In what areas of your life have you the most difficulty forgiving yourself for imperfection—for negative feelings or thoughts?

- What words did you choose to judge yourself with?

- Can you put a "statute of limitations" on your past failures? Which ones will you be willing to let go?

- The word "atonement" can be read as "at-one-ment," the desire to integrate the self and become at one with oneself. How can you make atonement for your feelings of malice or negativity, for which you may still be judging yourself?

June 10

....

*A*lways do right, this will gratify
some and astonish the rest.

—Mark Twain

_____

_____

_____

_____

_____

_____

_____

_____

_____

_____

_____

_____

_____

_____

_____

_____

_____

_____

June 11

....

> *The manner of giving is worth*
> *more that the gift.*
>
> —Pierre Corneille

"When I loved you it was
with the full knowledge
that I was loving a
clay pot"   T. D. Jakes

"Much like my shells —
It has flaws and faults,
cracks and crevices". but He
still loves us.

Jeremiah 31:3
"For long ago the Lord has said
to Israel: I have loved you, O
my people, with an everlasting
love: with loving kindness, I
have drawn you to me."

June 12

···

The great mind knows the
power of gentleness.

—Robert Browning

God is always there—
"He has held you through rough
places, trusting the strengths
of His arms to keep you through
the pains of life. It has been a
long ride, but He is still holding
on."

Do you need a healing? Ask
God; He loves you like a father
and He cares how you feel.

Sometimes I want God
to heal the way I feel
it should be done.
I forget that it may
not be the right time
or way. I tend to
forget how many

June 13

··

Cont.

> The day a person becomes a cynic is the
> day he loses his youth.
>
> —Marvin D. Levy

storms that He has
seen me through.
Please help me to
trust in Your ways.

Eph. 3 17-19
And I pray that Christ will be
more and more at home in your hearts,
living within you as you trust in
him. May your roots go down deep
into the soil of God's marvelous love;
and may you be able to understand, —
how Long, how wide, how deep
and how high His love really is,
and to experience this love for
yourselves, though it is so great
that you will never see the end
of it or fully know or understand
it And so at last you will
be filled up with God himself.

June 14

....

*The ideals which have always shone
before me and filled me with the joy of living
are goodness, beauty and truth.*

—Albert Einstein

June 15
....

It was at the workshop on our
school's suicide policy. The presenter
announced that we'd be there for five
hours! A groan rose from the group
who hadn't been told the length of
the in-service meeting. Just then, the PA
system crackled with the message that
there were five cars parked illegally
which had to be moved. Forty-six
people quickly rose and left.

—Teacher at conference in Gurnee, Ill.

People who are in authority, even those whose
authority is temporary, like guest speakers, would
do well to consider the meeting from the point of view
of the participants, who are rarely there voluntarily.
Yet we've so often seen the leader or the speaker fall in
love with the power of the position and with having a
captive audience. A kindness would be to be gentle
with one's authority, to be empathic about the needs
and concerns of those participating.

Being clear about the timing of the meeting, making
the meeting room comfortable and inviting, and keeping the meeting short and focused on the task at hand
are paths to kinder meetings. Make attendance volun-
tary. Participants will appreciate your effort to structure
it to be interactive, practical and paced so as not to be
a soporific.

Whenever humor is appropriate include it. Is there
time for people to reconnect and socialize at the beginning of the meeting? Does the meeting address the

needs of new members to be briefed on old business or new expectations?

- What are some of your pet peeves about meetings? Make a list. Ask some of your friends and colleagues for theirs.

- Plan a meeting that would eliminate your pet peeves and be respectful of people's time, needs and feelings. Share your plan with the "right people" who might be helped by your insights.

- People's feelings of powerlessness are a major source of irritation and discontent about meetings. How can you structure meetings so that those in attendance feel empowered?

June 16
....

> M an is honored for his wisdom,
> loved for his kindness.
>
> —S. Cohen, *Mishlé Agur*, 1803, 57

It is possible for parents to teach their children knowledge and skills. We do this all the time. We cannot teach our children wisdom, however. Wisdom is what we do with the knowledge and skills we have. It is a product of our choice to organize our resources and use them in ways that are sensible, appropriate and caring. Just so, we can teach our children the ways of kindness, which will always remain with them as choices they can make or not. Each day of their lives, our children will have to choose to use their knowledge and abilities wisely.

- We may feel awe for the wise person, but we feel love for those who are kind as well. How has this been true in your life? Whom do you know who is both wise and kind?

- If you had to make a tough choice to be either wise or kind, which would you choose and why?

- Sometimes our wisdom speaks to us and we ignore it—perhaps when we are driven by some unmet need. Write in your journal about a time when you feel that you ignored your own wise inner voice and what its consequences were.

- When your wise inner voice speaks to you, does it speak to you of kindness? Or compassion? What is it saying today?

June 17

....

When kindness has left people,
even for a few moments, we become afraid
of them, as if their reason had left them.

—Willa Cather

June 18

. . . .

Love is best.

—Robert Browning

June 19

....

*P*romises may get friends,
but it is performance that must
nurse and keep them.

—Owen Felltham

June 20
....

The heart has eyes the brain knows nothing of.

—Charles Parkhurst

_____

_____

_____

_____

_____

_____

_____

_____

_____

_____

_____

_____

_____

_____

_____

_____

_____

_____

June 21

....

*The happiest moments my
heart knows are those in which it is
pouring forth its affections to a
few esteemed characters.*

—Thomas Jefferson

June 22

....

Laughter is internal jogging and
we all need our exercise.

—Sidney B. Simon

Humor is becoming widely recognized as therapeutic. It relaxes us, allows us relief from stress and helps others to see us as more approachable and human. We value those precious moments when, in a difficult meeting, something funny happens and the tension suddenly disappears. Yet many of us would just wait for the humor to happen spontaneously, as though humor was like the weather, only to be experienced, not controlled.

Building humor into every day in a deliberate, thoughtful and planned manner may seem contrived to some—but not to us. We think humor is so very important, useful and especially fun, that it is essential to include it in our planning of work days and of our private lives.

Simply by expressing and acting on that intention, humor is brought more reliably into our lives. Because our family, friends and co-workers know that we value humor, they are much more likely to engage in it with us. Because we value humor and fun, we find ourselves subscribing to humor magazines and newspapers, renting funny movies, buying various props to use when we get silly at home or at work.

- Can humor be planned or must it be spontaneous? Can you think of some times when you've deliberately planned humor into your day?

- Do you see the value of including humor in your

life, in your work? Write in your journal about the role that humor plays in your family.

- Humor needs balance and taste in order to be a kindness. Too much humor or humor that comes at inappropriate moments can be destructive. Humor that depends on putdowns, racism, ageism, sexism or on someone being embarrassed certainly is no kindness. How do you handle it when humor is done poorly and seems to misfire?

June 23

....

If you do one a favor, remind him not of it.

—Elijah ben Raphael, *Travaah*, 18C

There is a purity to acts of kindness done selflessly, done simply for the joy that they bring. When the recipient of a kind act shows gratitude it may feel good to the giver, but it can, at times, take away a little of that pure pleasure that came from just the *doing* of it. Perhaps that's why Rabbi Moses Maimonides' famous list of the "levels of charity" gave such a high place for acts done anonymously, where the doer doesn't even know who the recipient may be. Some do kindnesses simply to reap gratitude. This may be a holdover from childhood, when we did so much to get our parents' approval. Perhaps the most grown up thing we can do is to give kindnesses in ways that do not obligate or even slightly embarrass the receiver.

- Have you ever known a "gratitude collector"? What feelings in you were or are engendered by that person?

- Have you ever *been* a gratitude collector? Where did that behavior come from in you? Did it bring you the results you wanted?

- Plan to do a quiet anonymous kindness. Record in your journal your planning process, what happened and how you felt about yourself, having done it.

- In what ways can you build quiet, anonymous, but consistent, kindnesses into the fabric of your life?

June 24

....

*The test of friendship is assistance
in adversity, and that, too,
unconditional assistance.*

—Mahatma Gandhi

_____

_____

_____

_____

_____

_____

_____

_____

_____

_____

_____

_____

_____

_____

_____

_____

June 25

A whole stack of memories will never
equal one little hope.

—Charles M. Schulz

I wonder how many women
realize that they have a father
who never sleeps nor slumbers.
He has assigned angels to
compass about you and to
ensure your safety. He will
spare no expense to insure
that you are safe. He will
not rest. He will arise with
healing in His wings. He will
come to you in a flash and stay
with you through the night.
He is the Everlasting Father.
He doesn't leave, He doesn't desert,
and He doesn't forsake you.
He is there. What you must
come to understand is that He
cares so much for you.
He wants you to have
all that you need

June 26

....

W*e have a limited number
of heart beats and we're in charge
of how we use them.*

—Peter Alsop

Jeremiah 8: 21-22
God loves so much !!

June 27

....

> *I believe in the intentional use
> of positive feedback.*
>
> —Matt Weinstein

_____

_____

_____

_____

_____

_____

_____

_____

_____

_____

_____

_____

_____

_____

_____

_____

_____

_____

_____

June 28

....

Bring joy to one person in
the morning and ease the pain of
another in the evening.

—Buddhist saying

June 29

• •

The clear-sighted do not rule the world,
but they sustain and console it.

—Agnes Kepplier

The ability to see fairly, to acknowledge the mix between good and bad in all people, and to set aside our prejudices is a rare gift. These people do not always rule the world, but their compassion and ultimate sense of fairness keep society moving forward.

- Why do you think compassion is important in society?
- What instances of compassion have you witnessed this month?
- What can you do to sustain the world?

June 30

···

*If we analyze our motives we will find
that they are made either of love or of fear.*

—Ralph Waldo Emerson

People often define the opposite of love as hate.
Actually, it is fear. Fear of the unknown is the greatest cause of wars between countries. We make enemies
because we are ignorant of their customs, of their likes
and dislikes, of who they *really* are.

If we take the time to truly learn about others, we
may come to love them and then, perhaps, relish in the
knowledge that we have taken a small step toward
global peace.

- How has fear acted as a motivating force in your
  life?

- What led up to your feeling afraid?

- How has love been a motivating force in your
  life? Describe your feelings and the circumstances
  in detail.

Summer

You will find as you look back
upon your life that the moments
when you have really lived, are the
moments when you have done
things in the spirit of love.
—HENRY DRUMMOND

The lazy days of summer provide good
balance for energy expended other
times of the year. Be grateful for this opportunity to come back to your center where
play, hope, giving and loving can generate
itself for another season. Let this summer be
the wellspring of the growth of your spirit.
Don't postpone those little acts of love.

July

July 1

•••

*The purpose in life is not to win.
The purpose in life is to grow and share.
When you come back to look on all
you have done in life, you will get more
satisfaction from the pleasure you have
brought into other people's lives than
you will from the times that you
outdid and defeated them.*

—Rabbi Harold Kushner

The two great themes of our civilization seem to be competition and cooperation. We are programmed, early in life, to see ourselves as competitors. The teacher runs a spelling bee. The test papers are returned and all of us compare grades, subtly marking each other on secret lists. I want to get the best grade in my class in order to please my parent. Getting on the honor roll would even be better. And I have to be the best on my team (and be on the best team) and constantly strive against some standard, externally imposed.

My school fights its old rival. My state competes for the new auto plant. My country doesn't want to be left behind in the global economy. The news blares, night after night, in an endless array of the world seen as competition.

Yet, within the team we talk about "team spirit" and about not "hot-dogging" it, making sure we play a team game, not an individual one. The corporation looks for team players who can "fit in." We see someone less fortunate and we cooperate by contributing something to help. We sing together in church to make a "joyful noise unto the Lord."

- When you choose competition instead of cooperation, are the consequences different for you? Does it make you feel closer to other people?

- Being a competitor implies winners and losers. Winners sometimes gloat or otherwise behave in ways that remove them from "ordinary" people. Has that been true for you?

- Losers sometimes engage in sulking, revenge behavior or withdrawal from others. Have you ever done these things?

- Are there any benefits for you in choosing the cooperation side of the game of life?

July 2

....

You are rich, though you do not know it.
You have wells of kindness within your
heart. At times man will bless you more for
a smile, a kindly glance, a gesture
of forgiveness, than for treasures of gold.

—Kabak, *BaMishol HaTazar*

I was in seventh grade and had joined the basketball team. I was trying to learn the game, but being so competitive and pushing myself so hard that I was truly getting in my own way, the striving wasn't helping me learn. I was frustrated and judging myself harshly. My teammate, Pam, noticed my struggle and said to me, "It will come. Follow my lead. You're doing okay. Don't be so hard on yourself." It was amazing how important those few words were to me. The sense of acceptance and of being valued by a teammate, despite my amateur performance, allowed me to slow down and gain skill at a reasonable pace. Years later, I still carry around gratitude in my heart to Pam, my teammate of so many years ago. And I express my gratitude by reaching out to others in much the same way.

- What words have been of personal comfort to you and brought you hopefulness when despair or frustration seemed to be winning?

- What words can you bring out of your "well of kindness" today and give to those you meet, work with or love?

- How do you measure your wealth? Is your well of kindness listed in your personal assessment of net worth?

July 3

....

*W*hoever hears a baby's
first laugh pays for the celebration of
their coming into the world.

—Navajo saying

_____

_____

_____

_____

_____

_____

_____

_____

_____

_____

_____

_____

_____

_____

_____

_____

July 4

●●●

*If we analyze our motives we will find that
they are made either of love or of fear.*

—Ralph Waldo Emerson

Deliberate Acts of Kindness
for the Fourth of July

As you celebrate America's Independence Day, it is a good time to think about what this holiday can symbolize for you and your family. It is a celebration of independence and of freedom. We can consider that freedom comes with responsibility. Thomas Jefferson said, "Eternal vigilance is the price of liberty." It is necessary that one be vigilant in the protection of our independence. We must guard against more than encroachments by foreign nations, but more importantly in today's world, against the subtle loss of freedom that comes when we enslave ourselves to addictions, to over-dependence on others, to being observers rather than actors in our own lives.

We might spend our Fourth of July celebrating independence by thinking about and even planning ways that we can foster independence and self-responsibility in our own lives, in our families, and in our local communities and businesses.

- Write to your congressional representatives with the idea that a tax credit be given to those who volunteer time, skills and energy to charitable purposes and organizations.

- Break the cycle of blame: When you are in less

than favorable circumstances, instead of seeking whom to blame, ask yourself, "In what ways am I even partly responsible for the situation as it is and what can I do about it now?"

- Teach others to avoid the cycle of blame, too. Teach your children, your co-workers, everyone you know about this idea. Fault-finding and blame-seeking are pointless wastes of time and energy. Instead of spending your resources inquiring, "Who spilt the milk?" it makes more sense to use your energy to work on how to clean up the broken glass and buy a new glass and more milk.

- Think about the freedoms that you enjoy. What is your personal responsibility for maintaining them? What are some things you can do to keep those freedoms fresh and secure?

- Freedom inevitably involves responsibility. Can you take personal responsibility for some problems, concerns or issues in your family, your business or your neighborhood? People who complain about the encroachment of big government in their lives may not see that government is often simply responding to problems that everyone else has been ignoring.

- Interpersonal discord is often referred to as "fireworks" as in, "When they started to discuss the children's report cards, the *fireworks* really went off!" Can you be responsible for the discord that you are (or have been) part of in your relationships? Can you make this a safe and sane Fourth of July by being responsible for lowering the conflict in the way you relate?

- Decide that in this year's elections you will not only vote, but you'll let the candidates know that you want a campaign that focuses on issues, not on personal attacks.

- Teach a child about the dangers of explosive fireworks. Take a stand against them. Then give a child a chance to enjoy the holiday by finding out where the nearest or best municipal fireworks display is going to be and taking the child (and several friends?) to the show.

- The Fourth of July is a day when thousands of immigrants become citizens at centers all over the country. Find out where the nearest naturalization ceremony is going to be held and attend it. Bring your family to celebrate with these Americans-by-choice. See how happy they are to take on the responsibilities of citizenship. See their tears of joy and take the opportunity to speak with some of them, and you'll discover that they prize and cherish what many native-born citizens take for granted.

- Put a flag up in front of your house and offer to do the same for a neighbor.

- If you have any control over who gets hired, who gets trained, who gets promoted at your place of work, think of your responsibility to help people at or near the bottom see that the American Dream is a possible one. Try to create clear career paths in your business so that everyone at work feels a sense of hope and ownership in America.

July 5

....

Kindness is the power that makes an intelligent response to the needs of the object of its affection.

—Unknown

_____

_____

_____

_____

_____

_____

_____

_____

_____

_____

_____

_____

_____

_____

_____

_____

July 6
....

> *The evidence seems clear:*
> *Friendship is the most universal of*
> *all interhuman relations in the emotional*
> *order. The simple and the advanced,*
> *criminals and saints taste its joys*
> *and find in it the means of*
> *overcoming their loneliness.*
>
> —Ignace Lepp

July 7

....

*L*ove conquers all things; let us too
surrender to Love.

—Virgil

_____

_____

_____

_____

_____

_____

_____

_____

_____

_____

_____

_____

_____

_____

_____

_____

_____

_____

July 8

··

> *When kindness or understanding*
> *happens unexpectedly, there is*
> *no greater delight.*
>
> —William Bolcom

The unexpected, unasked-for kindness is truly a special delight. It oftentimes comes to us when we are feeling low, depressed, lost or hopeless. It can restore our faith or our hope in a redeeming future. It can help us believe in our fellow humans once again.

- Today, can you make it your mission to bring this special joy to just one person? What would be the benefit to you? Who comes to mind?

- Think of someone who was the bringer of one of these experiences to you at some time. Contact that person, if possible, and thank them again. Your doing so will result in a ripple effect and much more kindness will be the result.

July 9

....

Though I be invested with sovereignty of earth and sea, I will make myself affable and accessible to the poorest.

—Philo Judaeus, *The Decalogue*

Noblesse oblige is the old, unstated contract between the commoners and royalty: In exchange for your elevation, you must show caring for even the least of your subjects. Many fabulously wealthy people have shown similar concern through charitable works. Wealthy and powerful people are often seen as being charitable simply for the good public relations or the tax advantages they may glean. We must remember that such endowments and good works began long before tax deductions!

- When you read of a big donation or the establishment of an endowment by a wealthy person, what is your reaction? Is there any cynicism in it?

- When you do an act of charity or make a donation, what are your motivations? Are you ever motivated solely by the tax deduction or by the good reputation it may bring you?

- Have you ever considered writing to the donor mentioned in a news story, with a letter of appreciation for the good you think they may have just done? What would be the impact of your letter?

July 10
....

No man is an Island,
entire of itself; every man is a piece
of the continent, a part of the main; if a
Clod be washed away by the Sea, Europe
is the less, as well as if a Manor of
thy friends or of thine own were; any
man's death diminishes me, because I am
involved in Mankind; and therefore
never send to know for whom the
bell tolls; it tolls for thee.

—John Donne, *Devotion*

July 11

....

Affiliation and kindness are the
sources of all happiness.

—Gordon Allport

_____

_____

_____

_____

_____

_____

_____

_____

_____

_____

_____

_____

_____

_____

_____

_____

_____

July 12
....

Altruistic children seem to be better
adjusted socially than others—they are less
aggressive, quarrelsome, and competitive,
and they are more emotionally stable.

—Dennis Krebs

_____

_____

_____

_____

_____

_____

_____

_____

_____

_____

_____

_____

_____

_____

_____

July 13

....

*If the world seems cold to you
kindle fires to warm it!*

—Lucy Larcom

July 14
....

> *Real strength is not just a condition*
> *of one's muscles, but a tenderness*
> *in one's spirit.*

—McCallister Dodds

_____

_____

_____

_____

_____

_____

_____

_____

_____

_____

_____

_____

_____

_____

_____

_____

_____

July 15

• •

*There are more things to admire
in man than to despise.*

—Albert Camus

Kindness ultimately comes from one's respect for others. People who are unable to value other people will probably have difficulty finding a reason to be kind. We all wear filters through which we view the world, the filters of our past experiences and what we've learned from them. Some of us, deeply wounded and embittered or fearful, see others as potential oppressors. Others may see the very same people as potential friends. Which pair of glasses do you wear?

- It's a challenge to be open (or to reopen oneself) to strangers or others who may trigger painful memories for us. What kinds of people trigger your defensive reactions?

- How do you cope with these reactions? Have you struggled to overcome them? Write in your journal about that struggle.

- Today is a day for lifting the veil, for putting down those filters and seeing someone in a new and fresh light. Who do you choose to do this with? What is it that this person was sent to teach you?

July 16

· ·

Help thy brother's boat across, and lo!
thine own has reached the shore.

—Hindu proverb

What we teach others we learn well ourselves. In the act of sharing one of your skills, it is amazing how much your own skill is honed and polished. We cannot think of a time that we've been helpful to others without gaining something powerfully positive from doing it.

- Think of a time you taught one of your skills or shared some knowledge. Write in your journal what you learned in the process.

- Who learned more, you or the person you taught?

- Consider thanking your "student" for the opportunity that she or he gave you to deepen your own knowledge.

July 17

....

God loveth a cheerful giver.

—St. Paul

_____

_____

_____

_____

_____

_____

_____

_____

_____

_____

_____

_____

_____

_____

_____

_____

_____

_____

July 18

··

> *The biggest disease today is not leprosy or tuberculosis, but rather the feeling of being unwanted.*
>
> —Mother Teresa

_____

_____

_____

_____

_____

_____

_____

_____

_____

_____

_____

_____

_____

_____

_____

July 19

··

*T*he world is round and the place which
may seem like the end may also be
the beginning.

—Ivy Baker Priest

_____

_____

_____

_____

_____

_____

_____

_____

_____

_____

_____

_____

_____

_____

_____

_____

July 20

....

Charity is injurious unless it helps the recipient to become independent of it.

—John D. Rockefeller

_____

_____

_____

_____

_____

_____

_____

_____

_____

_____

_____

_____

_____

_____

_____

_____

_____

_____

July 21

....

As *for doing good, that is one of
the professions that are full.*

—Henry David Thoreau

_____

_____

_____

_____

_____

_____

_____

_____

_____

_____

_____

_____

_____

_____

_____

_____

_____

_____

July 22

Those who bring sunshine to the lives of others cannot avoid it themselves.

—J.N. Barry

There's a glow of delight that comes to us when we are in the act of doing a kindness. Does it come from the other's gratitude or from the idea that someone else may learn of our good deed? Or could it come from some secret place inside where your inner voice says quietly, "Well done. That was a good thing to do. You're okay."

- Doing acts of kindness has an impact on our feelings. How do your own kindnesses affect you?

- We know people in a wide spectrum, from those who do kindnesses flamboyantly, hoping for and even asking for recognition for them, to someone who does kindnesses as a simple matter of lifetime habit and commitment and doesn't even think about them anymore, they're just so much a part of her. Where do you stand on that spectrum?

July 23

....

O*ur gifts and attainments*
are not only to be light and warmth in
our own dwellings, but are to shine
through the window, into the dark night,
to guide and cheer bewildered
travelers on the road.

—Henry Ward Beecher

We are all bewildered travelers on some sections of the road of our lives. Is there anyone alive who hasn't needed help or guidance at one time or another? We may feel alone and hopeless until a ray of kindness shines on us. We may be tempted, when we are doing the helping, to look down upon that lost traveler, forgetting we shared that perspective. Instead, see that person as someone needing help. See yourself.

- Kung Fu T'ze said, "The road of a thousand miles begins with a single step." Write in your journal about someone who helped you take a necessary first step.

- Wise counsel or just patient listening can be the help someone most needs. At other times, it can be listening to the story of *your* struggle with a similar problem. It is important to tell your story without pushing it as must-take advice.

- A company newsletter (or a family one) can be a great place for people to share stories of problems confronted and problems solved. Here the reader can learn problem-solving without having to share the problem publicly.

July 24

....

> We do not love people so much
> for the good they have done us, as for the
> good we have done them.
>
> —Leo Tolstoy

_____

_____

_____

_____

_____

_____

_____

_____

_____

_____

_____

_____

_____

_____

_____

_____

_____

_____

July 25

....

And learn the luxury of doing good.

—Oliver Goldsmith

_____

_____

_____

_____

_____

_____

_____

_____

_____

_____

_____

_____

_____

_____

_____

_____

July 26
....

*N*obody shoots at Santa Claus.

—Governor Al Smith

_____

_____

_____

_____

_____

_____

_____

_____

_____

_____

_____

_____

_____

_____

_____

_____

_____

_____

July 27

··

*I can live for two months on
a good compliment.*

—Mark Twain

_____

_____

_____

_____

_____

_____

_____

_____

_____

_____

_____

_____

_____

_____

_____

_____

_____

_____

July 28

> Certain thoughts are prayers. These are
> moments when, whatever be the attitude
> of the body, the soul is on its knees.

—Victor Hugo

Sr. Susan

July 29

W*here there is great love,*
there are always miracles.

—Willa Cather

L ove is a lifeline that pulls many a person from a hopeless situation. We sometimes read about accident victims, lost deep in a coma, who are sustained by their loved ones' hopes and prayers. The strength of this love can sometimes make the difference between life and death. With love, anything is possible.

- Think about the emotion of love. Rate its strength in relation to other emotions.
- What instances do you know of where love has created a miracle?
- Look in the newspaper for incidents like this and write them down in your journal.

July 30

....

*The best time for you to hold your tongue
is the time you feel you must say
something or bust.*

—Josh Billings

When we are entrusted with personal, confidential information about someone, we sometimes want to tell others. Betraying the trust, we ask the other person with whom we've shared the information to please not tell anyone else. And thus, rumors are spread.

A great act of kindness is to hold fast to our promise to keep confidential personal information about another. There is nothing to be gained from sharing this with others, no matter how "juicy" the subject matter.

- Think about your own most private, personal piece of information. How would you feel if this information was revealed to others?

- Do you remember a time when you betrayed someone else's trust? What did you gain from telling others this news? How did you feel afterward?

- Make a promise to yourself to keep secrets to yourself.

July 31

....

*T*ime invested in improving ourselves cuts
down on time wasted in disapproving
of others.

—Leona Green

August

August 1

···

> S*ympathy is two hearts*
> *tugging at one load.*
>
> —Charles Henry Parkhurst

O nce I worked for a wonderful and thoughtful man, Paul Benyei. I was struggling with the decision to ask my girlfriend to marry me. I vacillated wildly. "Should I? What if? . . . Suppose it doesn't work out?" All sorts of scenarios ran through my head. Since my boss was a close friend, I often would voice my doubts and fears.

One day, Paul said something that amazed me. "It's very hard to go through a life alone. You want some guarantee that this will be the perfect relationship with no problems? Sorry, there's no such thing to be had. You'll have to take a risk like the rest of us. But if it works, even for a period of time and not forever, that time will be uniquely happy for you. Pulling the wagon of life alone has been a crushing burden to me. Having a partner, even an imperfect one, or even being an imperfect one, but striving to really be a partner, that's made life bearable for me."

Paul gave me his sympathy, and in doing so, helped me tug at the load of my decision. I did marry. The marriage didn't last forever, but some of the best parts of my life happened in it. I learned some of my hardest and yet most important lessons in it. I had a partner to help me when my father died and my sadness seemed ready to drown me. "Thank you, Paul, wherever you are now."

- Do you believe that having a partner in life really helps in coping with life's burdens and travail?

- Have you been that partner who helped pull the load when it became a crushing one? How has that been for you?

- Is this something you can do for a friend as well as a mate? Is there a person in your life right now who might need your helping hand and loving heart?

August 2

....

> Kindness is the inability to
> remain at ease in the presence of
> another who is uncomfortable, the inability
> to have peace of mind when one's
> neighbor is troubled.
>
> —Samuel H. Holdenson

When children are kind, their kindness comes from sympathy, the human phenomenon of experiencing feelings similar to those of another. A higher level of maturity is to experience *empathy*, which is the ability to understand, accurately predict and to care about someone else's feelings or concerns. It is that "caring about" and the desire to do something about someone else's problems that distinguishes the informed heart.

- Can you remember some of your earliest experiences of empathy? Write about some of them in your journal.

- If you had the task of teaching empathy to children, without being preachy, how would you begin? Write your ideas in your journal.

- Share your ideas with your local elementary school or its parent-teacher organization.

August 3

. . . .

*True kindness presupposes the
faculty of imagining as one's own the
suffering and joy of others.*

—André Gide

_____

_____

_____

_____

_____

_____

_____

_____

_____

_____

_____

_____

_____

_____

_____

_____

August 4

....

The luxury of doing good surpasses
every other personal enjoyment.

—John Gay

_____

_____

_____

_____

_____

_____

_____

_____

_____

_____

_____

_____

_____

_____

_____

_____

_____

_____

August 5

....

*The greatest pleasure I know is to do a
good action by stealth, and to have
it found out by accident.*

—Charles Lamb

August 6
··

Die Tat ist alles, nichts der Ruhm.
(The deed is all, not the glory.)

—Johann Wolfgang von Goethe

_____

_____

_____

_____

_____

_____

_____

_____

_____

_____

_____

_____

_____

_____

_____

_____

_____

_____

August 7

....

"*He means well*" *is useless
unless he does well.*

—Titus Maccius Plautus

August 8

∙∙∙

> To make a sunrise in a place
> Where darkness reigned alone;
> That joy has never known;
> To plant a little happiness;
> In plots where weeds run riot—
> Takes very little time, and oh,
> It isn't hard—just try it!
>
> —Mary Carolyn Davies

You've said the right things, you sent the card. And yet you are aware that your friend's grief goes on. However, in the busy pattern of your life, there are so many things to do, calls to make, chores to finish. Because your own life is filled and your thoughts occupied with details and plans, it may be hard to remember the silence and emptiness the other person may be feeling, making each day seem like an eternity of tears. That extra note or phone call today, now, might be just what your friend needs to cope with her loss. Ask your friend for help! Involve your friend in the business of life. Show her that she's still needed. It's a kindness.

- List other ways of acknowledging your friend's loss or of reinvolving your friend in the business and busyness of life.

- When sadness and loss come into our lives, we can lose the motivation to keep things up, by doing the homely acts of maintenance that keep our lives in order. When a friend is grieving, volunteer to pick up their laundry, do their filing,

answer their mail, deal with their bills, do their
supermarket run.

- Write in your journal about your feelings for your
  friend, or about his or her loss. Or write about your
  own sense of loss in your life and what helped you
  cope with it.

August 9

••

> *Never promise more than*
> *you can deliver; instead deliver*
> *more than you promise.*
>
> —Gene Bedley

When our son Ethan was four, he overheard Hanoch on the phone. Hanoch was saying to a colleague, "Okay, Sam. Can I count on you? Fine. I'll see you tomorrow." When Hanoch hung up, Ethan asked, "Daddy, can I count on you?" Not knowing that Ethan was simply intrigued with the phrase, Hanoch said, "Sure you can, son, always." And Ethan proceeded to count on Hanoch, "One, two, three, four, five . . ." his fingers tapping out numbers on his father's arm. His childish delight with the silliness of the phrase when taken literally caused peals of joyous laughter for father and son.

- On whom can you count in your life? If you think about it and allow yourself the gift of a trusting heart, you'll find many names to put on your list. Make that list now, in your journal.

- Write a letter to one of the people on your list, with thanks for being a trustable resource in your life.

- Make another list of those who can (and do) count on you. Why not thank them for the gift of their trust?

August 10

· ·

Kindness has converted more sinners
than zeal, eloquence or learning.

—Frederick W. Faber

August 11

Much more genius is needed to be loving
than to command armies.

—Ninon do Lenclos

August 12

*It is better to love too many
than one too few.*

—Sir John Harington

August 13

A new commandment I give unto you,
that ye love one another.

—Jesus Christ

August 14

....

*K*indness is like a garden of blessing
   and love endures forever.

—Eccles. 40:17

August 15

···

> *Unless we cultivate tenderness,*
> *what will become of a human world*
> *that is now as red as nature in*
> *tooth and claw?*
>
> —Van Wyck Brooks

It's tempting and easy, if one watches the newscasts and reads the paper, to see only the brutishness, violence and greed that are daily reported to us so breathlessly. Is it really such a nasty world? One would be a fool to deny the hard facts of carjackings, murders, terrorism and war. Or to pretend that politicians aren't planning some new pandering legislation to establish orphanages or deny services to the poor. These things exist, have existed and will exist. Van Wyck Brooks reminds us that, if there is to be tenderness, empathy, loving kindness, concern for others, altruism in the world, it will not come by accident or magic. It is created, piece by piece and step by step, by just plain folks such as us. It is your deliberate decision to seek tenderness, act kindly, contend against cruelty that will redress the balances of the world we live in.

- Consider an issue in today's news that evokes an emotional response in you. Think about writing a letter of commendation instead of one of complaint. Write to someone about what's good in their actions or plans instead of what ought to be changed. Make positive suggestions instead of attacking their errors.

- Counter a negative rumor or bit of critical gossip by saying something positive and hopeful about the person or policy being discussed. What difference would that make?

- Look to the future: What policy or tradition can you work on, change or create that would bring more tenderness?

August 16

···

Each human brings to the world
his unique point of view. No one else can
ever have that particular vision and insight.
And, like fragile disappearing species
in the rapidly diminishing rainforests, when
one person dies, the world can never
again recover what he or she could have
contributed had there been time and
opportunity and someone
willing to listen.

—Hanoch McCarty

Consider a different point of view. It's a kindness to take someone else's point of view seriously and respectfully. It's courageous to do this even when you disagree. It also takes great patience, openness of spirit and maturity.

- If you always work from your own assumptions alone, you cut yourself off from learning anything new, discovering the limits of your thinking, achieving insight. Write about this in your journal.

- How can you help others in your family or at your workplace to open themselves in this way?

....

I shall pass through this world but once.
If, therefore, there be any kindness
I can show, or any good thing I can do, let
me do it now; let me not defer it or neglect
it, for I shall not pass this way again.

—Etienne de Grellet

August 18

*Wise sayings often fall on barren
ground; but a kind word is
never thrown away.*

—Arthur Helps

_____

_____

_____

_____

_____

_____

_____

_____

_____

_____

_____

_____

_____

_____

_____

_____

_____

_____

_____

_____

....

One kind word can warm
three winter months.

—Japanese proverb

_____

_____

_____

_____

_____

_____

_____

_____

_____

_____

_____

_____

_____

_____

_____

_____

_____

_____

August 20

···

> Kindness is the rule for
> everything she says.
>
> —Prov. 31:26

_____

_____

_____

_____

_____

_____

_____

_____

_____

_____

_____

_____

_____

_____

_____

_____

_____

_____

August 21

··

*It is a kindness to refuse gently
what you intend to deny.*

—Publius Syrus

_____

_____

_____

_____

_____

_____

_____

_____

_____

_____

_____

_____

_____

_____

_____

_____

August 22
....

Ben Franklin once said,
"To turn an enemy into a friend,
need something the other person can give.
For example, borrow a book only he may
have." I say, if you really want to make
someone happy, return their book
you borrowed so long ago!

—Janice Blackwill

Return a friend's favorite book. Add something to the exchange, like writing a note about what you gained from the book or similar experiences you've had. Or, perhaps you can buy another book on similar themes and include it. Best of all, you can invite your friend to dinner to discuss the book and what it's meant to both of you.

- Some friends are what we call "intelligence stretchers" because they challenge us to think new thoughts and entertain new ideas. What people in your life play this role for you? What do you find most interesting about these people?

- For whom are you an intelligence stretcher? For whom would you like to be?

- Create an opportunity to share ideas with one of these friends and share the idea of being an intelligence stretcher.

August 23

....

The unexpected gift, the little treat
that comes into your life almost magically,
can transform the most humdrum
day into a very special event.

—Meladee McCarty

Take a bag of fresh cookies or warm bagels to work today. Leave them near the coffee machine with a note that reads, "A gift from the Kindness Phantom." Don't let anyone know that you were the donor.

- Watch people's reactions. Write them in your journal.

- What feelings did you experience?

- Did your act of kindness spark any others from your co-workers or from you?

August 24

....

> Be kind. Remember everyone you
> meet is fighting a hard battle.
>
> —T.H. Thompson

_____

_____

_____

_____

_____

_____

_____

_____

_____

_____

_____

_____

_____

_____

_____

_____

_____

_____

August 25

••

*T*heir kindness cheer'd his drooping soul;
   And slowly down his wrinkled cheek
The big round tears were seen to roll,
   And told the thanks he could not speak.
The children, too, began to sigh,
   And all their merry chat was o'er,
And yet they felt, they knew not why,
   More glad than they had done before.

—Lucy Aiken, *The Beggar Man*

_____

_____

_____

_____

_____

_____

_____

_____

_____

_____

August 26

....

> *If you quit loving the moment it becomes difficult, you never discover compassion.*
>
> —David Augsburger

_____

_____

_____

_____

_____

_____

_____

_____

_____

_____

_____

_____

_____

_____

_____

_____

August 27
....

*There is no exercise better
for the heart than reaching down
and lifting people up.*

—John Andrew Homer

August 28

....

> *If we could read the secret
> history of our enemies, we should find
> in each man's life sorrow and suffering
> enough to disarm all hostility.*
>
> —Henry Wadsworth Longfellow

August 29

··

We grow a little every time we do not take advantage of somebody's weakness.

—Bern Williams

Each of us has strengths and weaknesses. It is the balance of life. Building on our strengths is a good goal—unless we target the weakness of another as our method of choice. Not only does this make our victories hollow, it can also belittle the other person. Focus, instead, on becoming the best person you can be.

- List your strengths.
- Now list your weaknesses.
- How can your strengths help you achieve your goals? Make a detailed plan.
- Choose a weakness that you would like to turn into a strength. Brainstorm ways you can do this.

August 30

> B*e kind to unkind people:*
> *they need it the most.*
>
> —Glennis Weatherall

Unkind people are not born that way. We cannot know the circumstances which turn a baby, born into the world sweet and innocent, into a hostile, grumpy adult. Sometimes they have endured physical and emotional abuse, or have been hardened by other unfortunate turns of events.

A natural reaction to an unkind word is to turn the other cheek. Say something nice back instead. You just might be surprised at the results!

- Who is the most unkind person you know? What do you know about that person's history? Empathize with him.

- What nice things can you say the next time you see him?

August 31
....

 C ompassion and kindness is the
       basis of all morality.

                              —Arthur Schopenhauer

_____

_____

_____

_____

_____

_____

_____

_____

_____

_____

_____

_____

_____

_____

_____

September

Deliberate Acts of Kindness
for Labor Day
(First Monday in September)

- Don't let your kindness be random. Random means occasional, accidental, ambiguous, unmotivated. Instead, make your kindness a deliberate, planned, systemic, thoughtful and consistent part of the way you do business in your office.

- Build in a concern for the physical health and safety of everyone in your workplace: the parking lot, getting to and from the office, smoking and other pollution, traffic patterns in the office, other health issues such as exercise, good food, ergonomic equipment.

- Build in a concern for the emotional health and safety of everyone in your workplace: freedom from ridicule and embarrassment, no sexual harassment, hopefulness, career paths and ladders, recognition of achievements, celebrating strengths and building on them, chances to grow and learn, use of appropriate humor, emphasis on cooperation, not competition.

- Commit to the use of *kind language* in your office. Focus on positives, on do's instead of don'ts. Learn to limit criticism. Soften the way you talk. Remove cussing, put-downs, critical comparisons. Remember that even *looks* are non-verbal words—and looks can kill. Refuse to engage in gossip, no matter how tempting. Ask people to stop if they are gossiping. Don't be part of racist, sexist or ageist language, jokes or behavior.

- Share success stories at staff meetings. Recognize people for their contributions. Choose to have a *can do* attitude. Always find the true dimensions of the problem. If someone says, "Our clients are all very upset that . . . " find out how many clients are being discussed. Keep rumor low and reality high.

- Commit to moving toward clear communication between staff members and with your clients. Ensure that your message has been heard. Use specific times, dates, amounts. Don't use vague words. Follow up on communication. Have handouts for your patients or clients that summarizes what you've told them.

- Send a thank-you note after a client visits your office—along with a reminder of the next appointment.

- Remember that angry clients may be wounded birds. Be understanding of their pain, sidestep their anger by telling yourself, "It's not aimed at me personally."

- Understand and enroll yourself in your office's "mission." What are you there for? What is your purpose (beyond the daily humdrum of appointments)? Remind yourself to bring every day's behavior in line with your deeper mission.

- Do your job with "quiet competence." Be fully who you are, with all your artistry, as though this day—this very day—was your chance to do the most perfect version of your job possible, to live yourself, and your profession, to the maximum.

- Keep confidentiality. When people confide in you, let them be absolutely sure that they have no need to worry about their news getting around. Make sure what goes on in your office stays in your office. Your clients will be very grateful.

September 1

....

Not all help is truly helpful.
When help consists of solving the
problem for someone, an unintended result
can be dependency and lowered
self-confidence. Real help insists that the
helpee do much of the work, nearly all of
the decision-making and lots of the
learning. It's more time-consuming and
challenging to be a real helper.

—Hanoch McCarty

Make a commitment to help someone in a way that leaves the person strong and more self-reliant. Give them the gift of your confidence in them. Let them know that you expect, and know, that they will succeed. Offer help in terms of empowerment, of skill development or of adding just that bit of information that allows them to take action on their own.

- Write about your urge to give advice and whether advice-giving is the most helpful thing you can do.

- If you could remove the sense of your own ego from your helping of others, how would that change your behavior?

September 2

....

*The Plains Indians believed
that each person has a "dreaming partner,"
someone who was fated to share dreams
and take them most seriously.*

—Hanoch McCarty

Share a goal or dream you hope to achieve. Tell it with your full artistry. Don't be afraid to be corny, sentimental or even naïve. It is a true kindness to have faith in your listener.

- Who do you think is your dreaming partner? Have you shared dreams with this person?

- How do you benefit from having a dreaming partner?

- In childhood there are often dreaming partners, others with whom you shared your fantasies, plans and secret hopes. Write to one of your childhood chums about the dreams you remember sharing. See where this takes you.

September 3

....

It is possible to give without loving, but it is impossible to love without giving.

—Richard Braunstein

_____

_____

_____

_____

_____

_____

_____

_____

_____

_____

_____

_____

_____

_____

_____

_____

_____

_____

September 4

....

Giving is a joy if we do it in
the right spirit. It all depends on whether
we think of it as "What can I spare?"
or as "What can I share?"

—Anonymous

September 5

··

We make a living by what we get, but
we make a life by what we give.

—Winston S. Churchill

September 6

....

We cannot exist as a little island of well-being in a world where two-thirds of the people go to bed hungry every night.

—Eleanor Roosevelt

September 7

....

Let everyone give as his heart
tells him, neither grudgingly nor under
compulsion, for God loves the man
who gives cheerfully. After all, God can
give you everything that you need,
so that you may always have sufficient
both for yourselves and for giving
away to other people.

—2 Cor. 9:7-8

September 8

....

*Best friend, my well-spring
in the wilderness!*

—George Eliot

Be the eyes and ears for your friends. If you know a friend is deeply interested in something, cut out all the articles you ever see about it and send them to him or her. Create a "tickler file" for each of your friends and stuff articles in them. Mail them once a month. Think about how valued each of them will feel.

- How do we remain "alive" to our friends? It is through consistent connection and through remaining engaged with the world. Think about how a tickler file would work to keep you alive to friends. Write about this in your journal.

- Think about browsing through antiques stores. Lots of beautiful objects, but your interest is piqued only when you choose to collect something. As a collector, your eyes scan the stores more alertly and knowingly. Keeping a tickler file for friends will change the way you read magazines and newspapers.

- Use this method to help a public official keep abreast of an issue important to you. Send him or her articles regularly. Will this make a difference?

September 9

∙∙∙

> B*e courteous to all, but intimate with
> few, and let those few be well tried before
> you give them your confidence. True
> friendship is a plant of slow growth,
> and must undergo and withstand the
> shocks of adversity before it is entitled
> to the appellation.*
>
> —George Washington

A book on counseling was titled something like, *The Purchase of Friendship*. The author likened a good therapist to a special friend who could be trusted to be a confidante. Your inmost sharings would be kept completely confidential. It is sad that many people have no one in whom to place such trust. Your act of kindness could be to cultivate the skills and commitment necessary to be a great confidante.

- Think of a time when you most needed someone in whom to confide. Write about that time in your journal. How did having a confidante help you?

- What is it that drives us to need a confidante?

- What is it about a person that inspires you to confide in him or her? What do *you* need to do to be seen in this way?

September 10

....

*Love is not only something you feel.
It's something you do.*

—David Wilkerson

September 11

Giving requires good sense.

—Ovid

September 12

....

*To cultivate kindness is a valuable
part of the business of life.*

—Samuel Johnson

_____

_____

_____

_____

_____

_____

_____

_____

_____

_____

_____

_____

_____

_____

_____

_____

_____

September 13

··

*Charity suffereth long, and is kind;
charity envieth not; charity vaunteth not
itself, is not puffed up.*

—1 Cor. 13:4

September 14

···

But how shall we expect
*charity toward others, when we are
uncharitable to our selves?*

—Sir Thomas Browne

September 15

....

> *Lose your sense of humor and you are truly lost.*
>
> —Ethan McCarty

Kindness can be found in *balance*. There will surely be enough seriousness and heavy times in every life, yours included. Strive to add a balance of lightness, of cheer and humor, and of seeing the hopeful, happy side of things.

- When was the last time you laughed so hard that your sides hurt? Write about that time in your journal. How did that laughter help clear your tension?

- You have a choice to just wait until the humorous event comes to you or you can plan to create such moments deliberately. Which will you choose?

- What is it that you can do today to bring lightness and humor to your day and to your friends and family?

September 16

··

*H*ome *is my refuge, my island of peace
in a striving, contentious world.*

—Victor Schmenge

On certain days, we may return home with energy spent, often carrying heavy weights of worry and stress. At that moment of return, think of your reaction if you found a sweet note, the gift of love and laughter from a friend. Leave a beautiful houseplant at a friend's door with a note that says "I'll always be *rooting* for you!"

- Which items do you associate with relaxation, relief from stress, or the creation of calm feelings? Which works best for you? A houseplant? A funny movie on video cassette? A book of tender poetry? It's time to arrange that your spouse or treasured friend have waiting at day's end whatever you think will help them relax. Write about his or her reaction in your journal.

- Imagine the delicious pleasure there is in planning end-of-day surprises for the people you care about. Talk about that with someone important to you. Create a loving conspiracy to do that for someone else.

September 17

··

Is she kind as she is fair?
For beauty lives with kindness.

—William Shakespeare

September 18

Have you had a kindness shown?
Pass it on!
Twas not given for thee alone,
Pass it on!
Let it travel down the years,
Let it wipe another's tears,
Till in Heaven the deed appears
Pass it on!

—Henry Burton

_____

_____

_____

_____

_____

_____

_____

_____

_____

_____

_____

_____

_____

_____

September 19

*Little deeds of kindness, little words
of love, help to make earth happy
like the heaven above.*

—Julia Carney

September 20

....

Good will is the mightiest practical
force in the universe.

—C.F. Dole

September 21

....

*Let me be a little kinder,
let me be a little blinder to the faults
of those around me.*

—Edgar A. Guest

_____

_____

_____

_____

_____

_____

_____

_____

_____

_____

_____

_____

_____

_____

_____

_____

_____

September 22

Not to decide, is to decide.

—Anonymous

In the summer of 1938 at Evian-les-Bains in France, a conference was held, sponsored by the League of Nations, to discuss the plight of the Jews and others in Nazi Germany. The delegates assembled and chose not to do anything since "it was an internal matter" for Germany. The Nazis, who had been worried about international opinion, were encouraged by this response and decided to go ahead with their plans for the Holocaust.

Raising your single voice when you know some wrong needs righting, has the potential for an impact far beyond your expectations. Each voice is noted.

- Is there a wrong that needs righting that you know about? Write about it in your journal.

- Raising a voice can mean: 1. writing letters to editors or members of Congress, 2. carrying a picket sign, 3. collecting money or items that are needed, 4. volunteering your time, 5. marching for, or against, a cause. Which of these matches your style? Write about how you might help the cause of your choice.

- Send that letter, make that call, prepare that sign, volunteer that time.

September 23

● ●

If you want others to be happy, practice compassion; if you want to be happy, practice compassion.

—Anonymous

Today is the day to drop an old grudge you've been carrying. Lighten your load by letting go. Replace it with something sweet—a newer, sweeter memory. Don't wait for the apology. Don't wait for some compensation from the other person. Dropping a grudge feels better when you've decided to do it unilaterally, simply because it's the right thing to do.

- Are you carrying any old grudges? Look inside and find them if they are there. How much do they weigh? At what cost are you carrying them? Write about this in your journal.

- What would you gain by dropping some of them? What would the other person, or persons, gain?

- Dropping a grudge is always a unilateral act. You don't have to wait for some sign from the other side. What are you waiting for?

September 24

....

K*indness is the sunshine in*
which virtue grows.

—Robert G. Ingersoll

September 25
....

> *The kindness I have longest*
> *remembered has been of this sort, the*
> *sort unsaid; so far behind the speaker's lips*
> *and that almost it already lay in my heart.*
> *It did not have far to go to*
> *be communicated.*

—Henry David Thoreau

September 26

....

So many gods, so many creeds,
so many paths that wind and wind, while
just the art of being kind is all
the sad world needs.

—Ella Wheeler Wilcox

September 27

....

> What you give for the cause of
> charity in health is gold; what you give
> in sickness is silver; what you
> give after death is lead.
>
> —Jewish proverb

September 28

....

*B*ehold, I do not give lectures or a little
charity, when I give I give myself.

—Walt Whitman

_____

_____

_____

_____

_____

_____

_____

_____

_____

_____

_____

_____

_____

_____

_____

_____

_____

September 29
....

> You get the best out of others when you
> give the best of yourself.
>
> —Henry Firestone

Lead by example. If you are weary of pessimistic behavior from co-workers, vow not to join in the complaining-at-the-watercooler club. Instead, be optimistic and do your job the best you can. Not only will you feel and perform better, you may just inspire others around you to perform at their peak.

- What are the major "gripes" around your office? Are they legitimate? If so, what can you do to improve the situation?

- List your greatest strength at work. Write down ways to channel this into improved work performance.

- How can you help others with their performance?

September 30

....

It is the experience of living that is important, not searching for meaning. We bring meaning by how we love the world.

—Bernie Siegel, M.D.

Paying lip service to spirituality means nothing. We may read all we want about lofty ideas, such as the meaning of life, but if we don't find it in our hearts to act with kindness and compassion in everyday encounters, the words are wasted.

- Take an inventory of the most important people in your life.

- Write down the milestones in your life. How did these events change you? What did you learn?

Fall

I n the fall we look forward to the change of temperatures, the falling leaves, the harvesting of our resources. In order to keep our lands fertile we must replenish them, give back to them and nurture their renewal. So it is with humans, we need to replenish ourselves and those we come in contact with.

There is one word which may serve as a rule of practice for all one's life—reciprocity.

—CONFUCIUS

October

October 1

Soft voices invite soft replies, hard voices invite hard replies.

—Laura Spiess

Give someone a soft answer today when a harsh reply might have been your response. Choose to de-escalate the encounter. Choose silence when that seems right.

- Anger seems to be the result when our ego gets hurt. Is ego a player in the game of your life?

- What would be the cost to you to choose the soft response instead of the hard one?

- What are some words you can choose that would feel softer, less confrontational, more accepting and less likely to produce more anger?

October 2

．．．

*Happiness is when what
you think, what you say, and what
you do are in harmony.*

—Mahatma Gandhi

It is kindness to the self to be in harmony. There is a tearing feeling we experience when our behavior is at variance with the voices inside us that speak of our values and tell us right from wrong. Your essence is expressed by this harmony.

- Think of the times that you felt most in harmony with your inner self. Write about this in your journal.

- When you are in this state of harmony, you are a most attractive model to others. For whom do you serve as a model?

- What can you do to help yourself and others be more frequently in harmony?

October 3

....

*There is no beautifier of
complexion, or form, or behavior,
like the wish to scatter joy and
not pain around us.*

—Ralph Waldo Emerson

_____

_____

_____

_____

_____

_____

_____

_____

_____

_____

_____

_____

_____

_____

October 4

*The hands that help are holier
than the lips that pray.*

—Robert G. Ingersoll

_____

_____

_____

_____

_____

_____

_____

_____

_____

_____

_____

_____

_____

_____

_____

_____

_____

October 5

....

*To pity distress is but human;
to relive it is Godlike.*

—Horace Mann

October 6

....

He saw the goodness, not the taint,
in many a poor, do-nothing creature, and
gave to sinner and to saint, but kept
his faith in human nature.

—Horace Greeley

October 7
....

> You can't get rid of poverty by
> giving people money.
>
> —P.J. O'Rourke

_____

_____

_____

_____

_____

_____

_____

_____

_____

_____

_____

_____

_____

_____

_____

_____

_____

_____

October 8

....

There is no medicine like hope,
no incentive so great, and no tonic so
powerful as expectation of
something tomorrow.

—O.S. Marden

Tell someone of a great failure you've had and how you overcame it. Failure stories can be great sources of hope since they illustrate that: (1) we can survive failure and (2) we are not alone when we've failed.

- Are there people in your life who have offered you hopefulness? What were their comforting words to you?

- In what ways could you use those comforting words to put things in perspective for another person?

- How can you encourage others to spread hope in the world?

October 9

....

> A *sense of humor can help you overlook*
> *the unattractive, tolerate the unpleasant,*
> *cope with the unexpected, and smile*
> *through the most unbearable.*
>
> —Moshe Waldoks

Forgive an injustice. Work with another person to explore the lighter and more acceptable alternative to a problem. Sometimes a person's unjust behavior comes from their not seeing what else they could have done and focusing only on the gravity of the situation.

- Stepping back from being a judge and deciding to forgive isn't easy. Looking for some humor in the situation can help you let go of the judge's role.

- Remind yourself of some of your own flaws, mistakes, poor choices. Think of some that were, in retrospect, particularly funny. Allow yourself to see your kinship with someone who has also made a big error. Share your new insight with them.

October 10

....

*We ought to think that we are
one of the leaves of a tree, and the tree is
all humanity. We cannot live without
the others, without the tree.*

—Pablo Casals

October 11

··

*From what we get, we can make a living;
what we give, however, makes a life.*

—Arthur Ashe

_____

_____

_____

_____

_____

_____

_____

_____

_____

_____

_____

_____

_____

_____

_____

_____

October 12

In any contest between power and
patience, bet on patience.

—W.B. Prescott

October 13

....

> At different stages of our lives,
> the signs of love may vary, dependence,
> attraction, contentment, worry, loyalty,
> grief, but at heart, the source is always the
> same. Human beings have the rare
> capacity to connect with each
> other, against all odds.

—Michael Dorris

October 14

You never know what little
bundle of encouragements artists carry
around with them, what little pats on the
back from what hands, what newspaper
clipping, what word of hope from what
teacher. I suppose that the so-called faith in
ourselves is the foundation of our talent,
but I am sure these encouragements are
the mortar that holds it together.

—Luciano Pavarotti

_____

_____

_____

_____

_____

_____

_____

_____

_____

_____

_____

_____

October 15

· ·

> Cancer is probably the most
> unfunny thing in the world. But I'm
> a comedienne, and even cancer couldn't
> stop me from seeing humor in
> what I went through.
>
> —Gilda Radner

Read something uplifting to someone. Let yourself listen to it too. Search for uplifting things to read. The search alone will be worth the effort. In your quest for the lighter side, the meaningful, the humorous, the redeeming message, there will be a serendipity that will ensure that you'll find much more than you ever imagined. Share that richness with those you prize and cherish.

- Words can be nourishing. They can be *vitamins* for your spirit. Think of some words that have touched your heart. Find them again and share them.

- Search for quotes of joy, hope and light. Start a file for them. Copy them onto index cards and put them around your life, on dashboards, bathroom mirrors, computer monitor and office walls. Allow yourself to be sentimental and upbeat.

- Who needs a copy of these great quotes you've found? Hit the copy machine and then run to the mailbox!

October 16

....

*If there is no malice in your heart,
there can be none in your jokes.*

—Will Rogers

Humor helps us to relieve tension while finding the lighter side of things. Yet sometimes the "dark side of the Force" enters our humor through put-downs, racism, sexism and the like. Sarcasm may be anger expressed with a smile. Such jokes open distance rather than create healing.

- Examine your use of humor. Are there parts of your humor that might be better left out?

- What do you choose to laugh at? We continue negative humor by making an audience for it. Without becoming the Political Correctness Police, can you find a way to refrain from that kind of humor?

October 17

....

For kindness is a Mine, when great and true,
  Of Nobler Ore than even Indians knew;
  'Tis all that Mortals can on Heav'n bestow,
  And all that Heav'n can value here below.

—Katherine Fowler Phillips

October 18

Happy would it be for the
animal creation, if every human being . . .
consulted the welfare of inferior creatures,
and neither spoiled them by indulgence,
nor injured them by tyranny!
Happy would mankind be . . .
by cultivating in their own minds and
those of their own children, the divine
principle of general benevolence.

—Favulus,
Histories: Or the History of the Robins

October 19

....

*E*very living creature that comes
into the world has something allotted
him to perform, therefore he should
not stand an idle spectator of
what others are doing.

—Sarah Kirby Tremmer

October 20

....

The man who lives by himself and for himself is likely to be corrupted by the company he keeps.

—Charles H. Parkhurst

October 21

....

Kindness and generosity . . . *form the
true morality of human actions.*

—Germaine de Stael,
Reflections of the Moral Aim of Delphine

October 22

....

> Die when we may, I want it
> said of me, by those who knew me best,
> that I always plucked a thistle and
> planted a flower, when I thought
> a flower would grow.
>
> —Abraham Lincoln

Deliberate and thoughtful kindness, the kindness that is systematically built into one's life, is often characterized by the inability to walk past problems. Taking this approach to life causes one to assume responsibility when others pretend not to notice that something is amiss. The deliberately, habitually kind person picks the thistle so the next person doesn't get stuck, and plants the flower to leave a trail of beauty.

- Lincoln was concerned with his obituary. What would you like said about you after you are gone? Macabre though it may seem, some people have found that writing their own obituary helped to focus their values and their choices in life. Is this something you'd like to try in your journal?

- Teachers, psychologists, doctors, etc., are said to be part of *the helping professions*, sometimes called *meliorists*. Are you a meliorist in the way you live your life and respond to the world?

October 23

••

> N*ot all kindnesses are obvious. To see the kindness may take considerable thought.*
>
> —Hanoch McCarty

W*hen* he picked me up at the airport, John was cordial and excited about the workshop I was to do for his company that afternoon. He shared a stream of information about the group I would be working with and their particular interests. He said, "You'll find Carl an *experience!*" Carl was his boss and my host at the conference. "Carl is very overweight; he's huge," he continued. "Then there's Carl's way. He'll come on strong to you; he'll have opinions and may not listen very well. But I want you to know that Carl is not only my boss, he's my very good friend. And he's the glue that holds our company together."

It took me a while to see that this was an act of friendship and kindness. John prevented my embarrassment at meeting Carl by preparing me. Instead of being surprised, I was ready. Carl was a special case, and I learned swiftly how to work with him.

- Does this seem like a kindness to you or as simply talking behind someone's back? Would you do something like this?

- John gave a lot of thought to how to prevent conflict in his work place. What other ways have you tried?

- John also helped me to cope with a difficult situation by giving me information that altered the way the situation would look. Can you think of other ways you could help visitors and new people in your job?

October 24

....

*K*ind words don't wear out the tongue.

—Douglas Lawrence Bendell

October 25

••

Love is not getting, but giving.
It is sacrifice. And sacrifice is glorious!
I have no patience with women who
measure and weigh their love like a
country doctor dispensing capsules.
If a man is worth loving at all, he is worth
loving generously, even recklessly.

—Marie Dressler

_____

_____

_____

_____

_____

_____

_____

_____

_____

_____

_____

_____

October 26

....

*If you stop to be kind, you must
swerve often from your path.*

—Mary Webb

_____

_____

_____

_____

_____

_____

_____

_____

_____

_____

_____

_____

_____

_____

_____

_____

_____

_____

October 27

....

I think women need kindness more than love. When one human being is kind to another it's a very deep matter.

—Alice Childress

October 28

....

Moments of kindness and
reconciliation are worth having, even if the
parting has to come sooner or later.

—Alice Munro

October 29

· ·

A *friend is someone who*
knows your song, and sings it to
you when you forget.

—Eric Spiess

Help someone remember the good they've done, the talent they possess and their value to you. We sometimes think good thoughts without sharing them because we believe it's obvious that we feel that way. The other person, lacking ESP, may forever think you didn't care or judged them more harshly than you really did.

- Negative experiences can erase our appreciation of our self-worth. We can lose sight of the good in our lives. Do you have a friend who needs reminding of his/her value?

- Get in touch with the warm feelings, the sense of closeness you have experienced when reminding someone of their value in your life. Do you remember how soft they became at that moment? Write about this in your journal.

- We all wear some masks that we've painstakingly designed to help make us more acceptable to others. Sadly, these masks also distance us from them. At those moments when we affirm others, often the masks slip away and our souls connect. What can you do to have more of these moments in your life?

October 30

....

There is a reason for all things.
Faith means we don't always have
to have the answer.

—Petey Parker

When in the midst of a crisis—the death of a loved one, the loss of a job—it is difficult to believe that the event happened for a good reason. It is okay to admit we can't see the reason for the situation. At these difficult times, we should pay attention to showing ourselves kindness and allow ourselves to feel sad. Do something nice for yourself, and keep the faith that better days are on the way.

- Define faith. What role does faith play in your life?

- Think of a painful event that happened to you in the past. Write a personal essay about it and explain how you grew from it.

October 31

....

Deliberate Acts of Kindness
for Halloween

Halloween is one of those uniquely American holidays that began as a Christian religious cele-bration (All Hallows' Eve) and which has become more secular than religious in nature. Today, this is an evening dedicated to children, to fun and just being silly.

Some communities have had problems associated with Halloween—multiple incidences of arson in towns where the holiday is also called, "Devil's Night," and candies and fruit containing poison, needles or razor blades. It is unfortunate that our society has engendered such fearsome problems on an occasion which should be sweet for children and others. The following tips can help you make this a deliberately kinder Halloween:

- Keep your Halloween safe for children and adults in your community by supporting the local school carnival or "haunted fun house."

- Gather together some neighbors and begin your own community response to keep Halloween safe. Become a liaison with local schools. Present assem-blies about appropriate behavior for the holiday. Invite lots of parent support and participation.

- Take pictures of "trick or treaters" that you know from your neighborhood. Put them in an album to be shared year after year.

- Plan something unrelated to school work at your local school for students who do not participate in the holiday. Ensure that the project will bring out their creativity and talents so that it doesn't become a punishment to refrain from observing the holiday.

- Dress up for your workplace unless it is prohibited. Give yourself permission to act out the drama of your costume. Example: Dress as a fortune teller and tell everyone's fortune in a playful way. Include a prediction for a prosperous future in the company.

- Make up a bag of tricks to be handed out to the adults who come to your home accompanying their children. A kit might include a clown nose, silly glasses, an animal nose, bubbles, bright red wax lips or Dracula teeth.

- Leave messages for your family around the house from famous Halloween movies. Examples: "Your barber/hair stylist called and said it's time for you to come in for a trim," Wolf Man. "It's time to donate blood," Dracula. "It came to me like a bolt out of the blue; I love you," Frankenstein. "Come and watch a late night movie with me and snuggle," Vampira.

- Invite a friend who is a senior citizen to help hand out Halloween candy at your house. Serve a dessert he or she can enjoy.

- Put together a "haunted yard" for the kids in your neighborhood. Better yet, have them help you plan and put it together.

- Our late friend, Gene Borges, donned Captain Hook attire, decorated his riding lawn mower as a pirate ship towing a little red wagon, and drove all the two- to four-year-olds around his neighborhood to trick or treat.

- Make and deliver Halloween masks to your local "Meals on Wheels" so that home-bound people can get in on the fun. A good chuckle goes a long way to reduce stress and to help someone feel included.

November

Deliberate Acts of Kindness
for Thanksgiving
(Fourth Thursday in November)

Thanksgiving is the national holiday people associate most with families gathering together, returning from far-flung places to renew, reconnect and rejoice. It is a time of great joy and happiness, for which people spend a considerable amount of time and effort preparing for the feast and the family. It is an opportunity to count one's blessings and to give thanks for all that has been granted to you. There is something profoundly spiritual about this holiday, at least in the *idea* of Thanksgiving. All will depend on how each family approaches this special day.

Thanksgiving is also a time when tempers may flare ("Get out of my kitchen while I'm cooking! Go clean your room!"), and loneliness seems to peak for those who no longer have a family to be with and those who have been alienated from them. The constant reminders on TV of family feasts bring them only depression and sadness. In other families, competition may rear its ugly head, and spiteful comments and comparisons can remove the joy from the day in a flash of hurt or anger.

This is a moment in the year when it's important to ask yourself three very central questions:

- What do I want to *do* for Thanksgiving? Do I want to have the family over or go to Mom's house for dinner? Do I want to travel so far to be together with them? Do I dare miss this chance to be together, knowing that all of us may not be alive for next year's Thanksgiving?

- What do I want to *get* from this Thanksgiving? Is this holiday simply an excuse for overeating? Is the meal the important thing or is the gathering together of family and friends the central idea? Do I want to get closer to anyone in my family? Do I want to experience a feeling of closeness and communion with God? Do I want to express my gratitude for all the good in my life?

- How do I have to *be* in order to get what I want? There is a direct relationship between my choice of attitude and behavior during this holiday and the likely outcomes I will achieve. If I focus on the meal and its preparation to the exclusion of the feelings and needs of my family, I am more likely to be curt, impatient or rude to them and much less likely to become closer to them.

Some deliberate acts of kindness for Thanksgiving include:

- Prepare for the holiday in a way that includes your immediate family and allows each member to contribute. Resolve to be with them in a gentle, relaxed and caring way so that the process of preparation is as nourishing as the meal will be.

- Express your gratitude to the one you've lived with and loved. Tell him or her how thankful you are for their presence in your life.

- Think of your best teachers, your best guidance counselors or coaches. Take a moment to write a letter of appreciation to those who stand out in your memory because of their impact on you. If you have children, share your letter of thanks with them, too.

- If you've ever been in an accident or other life-threatening experience and were helped by an emergency medical technician, a fire-fighter, a nurse or doctor in an Emergency Room, invite them and their spouses to your celebration. Or throw a party in their honor to truly give thanks.

- Model thankfulness for your children. Gently, but firmly, insist that they send thank-you notes for gifts, and that they express gratefulness to those who help them.

- Do you have an old friend whom you have not seen or spoken with in years? This year, find this person and call or write to let them know how important they have been to you. You might revive that sweet old friendship and bring much joy.

- There are many people who cannot be with their families this year for the holiday. Invite some of them to your table. A call to the nearest armed forces base, to your church or synagogue, or a nearby college will yield many such people. Do you know someone who's experienced the death of a spouse or a parent or has been recently divorced? They might be very happy to be invited.

- Try the "Two-For-One Thanksgiving Plan." If you can afford it, as you shop for your turkey and trimmings, purchase two of everything. Pack the duplicates separately. On the way home, stop at a soup kitchen or a homeless shelter and drop off that second set of packages. You will know as you eat your meal that someone less fortunate is eating just as well as you are this year.

Thankfulness sets in motion a chain reaction that transforms people all around us, including ourselves. For no one ever misunderstands the melody of a grateful heart. Its message is universal, its lyrics transcend all earthly barriers; its music touches the heavens.

—Fred Bauer

November 1

....

*Small tokens of love carry messages
     far beyond their size.*

—Karl-Hans von Fremde

M ake up a "care package" for someone you know or
love who is traveling. Put in it special little
things that will make your friend feel especially cared
for: fresh fruit, gourmet cookies, the latest novel by
his/her favorite author, batteries for a portable stereo,
bandages for boo-boos, antacid tablets, any little thing
you think your traveler might appreciate. Enclose a
loving note and a picture of yourself.

- When you're on the road, it's easy to feel discon-
  nected, alienated or disoriented. Have you ever
  received a care package in those circumstances?
  How did it feel?

- Brainstorm with a friend or two, a whole panoply
  of small items that might go into a care package.
  This exercise will be fun and will increase your
  fund of ideas.

- What else might a traveler need?

November 2

· ·

W*hat's in it for me?*

It would be nice if all kindnesses were done simply because "it's the right thing to do." An astonishing amount *is* done for that reason. Kindness is truly its own reward, for people almost universally report that they feel better about themselves when they do acts of kindness. And cynics find it so hard to believe that people have done good with no thought of reward or return. "What goes around, comes around," they'll say. "He's just hoping to be rewarded somehow, some time." Motivation is much more complex than they expect. Perhaps most of us *do* have a little angel sitting on our shoulder whispering in our ear to do good works. What about you?

- What do you think? Is kindness a bit sappy? Do you believe that most people are simply out for themselves? What has your experience been like?

- This week, clip every newspaper article in which a person has performed an act of kindness. Count how many you collect in a week. Ask yourself what their motivations were.

November 3

....

"*I* think everything has value,
absolute value, a child, a house, a day's
work, the sky. But nothing will save us.
We were never meant to be saved."
"What were we meant for then?"
"To love the whole damned world."

—Jane Rule, *Desert of the Heart*

November 4

....

> *The source of justice is not vengeance but charity.*
>
> —Bridget of Sweden

November 5

....

"*L*ove worketh no ill to his neighbour,"
*therefore, if you have true benevolence,
you will never do anything injurious to
individuals, or to society.*

—Hester Chapone

November 6

....

> "It is quite fitting that charity
> should begin at home," said Wright;
> "but then it should not end at home;
> For those that help nobody will find none
> to help them in time of need."
>
> —Maria Edgeworth

_____

_____

_____

_____

_____

_____

_____

_____

_____

_____

_____

_____

_____

November 7

....

A mature person is one who
does not think only in absolutes, who is
able to be objective even when deeply
stirred emotionally, who has learned that
there is both good and bad in all people and
in all things, and who walks humbly and
deals charitably with the circumstances
of life, knowing therefore all of us
need both love and charity.

—Eleanor Roosevelt

November 8
....

> *L*ittle acts of kindness are stowed
> away in the heart like bags of lavender
> in a drawer to sweeten every
> object around them.
>
> —Laura Spiess

Smiles, like angry looks, are contagious. Watch what happens when a person enters a room with a smile or with an angry frown. The other people present, almost invariably, will respond in kind. Your little act of kindness brings a contagious smile to the faces of its recipients and a desire to pass on the good feelings to someone else as well.

- Humans are filled with energy. Thoughts and feelings are focuses for that energy. If you think about a sad experience, you will become sadder and your energy will fade. If you focus on anger, it will dominate. Try an experiment: Focus on one strong feeling you've had recently. Notice your responses to your own thoughts. What do you learn?

- Think about an act of kindness that was done for you at some time. As you think about it, what feelings occur to you? How does this affect your level of energy? As you think about it more, does it change the way you experience the world at this moment?

- Perform a deliberate act of kindness and watch its effects on its recipient. Can you see its effects? Do you change the world, even a little bit, and the potential for goodness, by your acts?

November 9

....

*K*indness in ourselves is
the honey that blunts the sting of
unkindness in another.

—Walter Savage Landor

I t often takes an effort of will to prevent oneself from
merely replying in kind when faced with another's
rudeness. "Oh, that's the way they're going to be, eh?
Well, I'll just . . ." The almost automatic mimicking of
the other person's behavior is probably rooted in childhood's many experiences of give and take, of defending
oneself from bullies and teasing. The bulwark of the
more adult response of deciding to return good for bad,
the source of this strength, is the habit of kindness.
Kindness must be cultivated as a habit, practiced in all
its forms in the regular course of one's life, to develop
into an automatic response. It seems very like develop-
ing strong muscles.

- What would "kindness aerobics" look like? Try to
  develop a daily practice of kindnesses, a regular
  kindness exercise plan.

- When faced with someone's rudeness or perhaps
  deliberate cruelty, you can choose to remind yourself of your choices at that moment; to copy the
  cruelty or to live your own values. You can also
  consider the source of the other's misguided
  behavior and feel compassion. Write about this in
  your journal.

November 10

· ·

It is not fair to ask of others what you are not willing to do yourself.

—Eleanor Roosevelt

November 11

....

Deliberate Acts of Kindness
for Veterans' Day

*Those who expect to reap the
blessings of freedom must undergo the
fatigue of supporting it.*

—Thomas Paine

*In every community, there is
work to be done. In every nation, there
are wounds to heal. In every heart,
there is the power to do it.*

—Marianne Williamson

*Responsibilities gravitate to the person
who can shoulder them.*

—Elbert Hubbart

The horrors of war touch every American family. And yet we continue to be the most altruistic country in the world, giving of our resources and ourselves, time and time again, even to former foes.

History repeats itself in war. Throughout the generations of our country, there have been countless stories of unconditional and heroic acts of kindness and courage. If you have the opportunity to visit the Vietnam War Memorial you will see people at all hours of the day and night coming to pay their respects, remember, heal and connect with one another. If you interview those present, you will hear countless stories of selfless kindness: from the nurse who looks for the soldier whom she helped to bring back from the grip of death, to the buddy who promised to tell his dying friend's family of his last words.

True heroism is remarkably sober, very undramatic. It is not the urge to surpass all others at whatever cost, but the urge to serve others at whatever cost.

—Arthur Ashe

All Americans can:

- Take responsibility for what we've reaped from our veterans' selfless acts of heroism by voting that they maintain their health care and mental health care privileges throughout their lives.

- Honor those veterans in your community on their day by publishing their names in the local paper, including where, and when, they served.

- Read the Declaration of Independence to your children on Veteran's Day and discuss with them how our freedom is a gift from America's veterans.

- Wear a yellow ribbon on this day to commemorate all those veterans who were lost in wars and were unable to return to their homeland.

- If you have a family member who served in one of our nation's wars or was a civilian who contributed to the war effort in some sort of supportive capacity, keep his or her story alive by sharing it with your children or other American youths. Don't let the story of the significance of this veteran's unconditional kindness and courage end with you.

November 12

∙∙

Charity. To love human beings insofar as they are nothing. That is to love them as God does.

—Simone Weil

November 13

....

Love appears every day for one who offers love, that wisdom is enough.

—Hadewijch

November 14

....

Accustom yourself continually
to make many acts of love, for they
enkindle and melt the soul.

—St. Teresa of Avila

November 15

> You have no tenderness, you have only justice, and therefore you are unjust.
>
> —Feodor Dostoevski

> Tenderness is total love, whereas justice is only a part of love, though it believes itself, mistakenly, to be the whole.
>
> —C.F. Ramuzt

Recently, in a now infamous court case, the adoptive parents of a four-year-old boy lost custody of the child to his birth mother, who had given him away, and to the biological father who had been told the child was dead. A four-year court battle ended when the little child was ripped away from the only parents he'd ever known because of "property rights" that birth parents seem to have. Lost in this story of the terrible beauty of justice is this little lad, who psychologists and social workers agree is likely to be permanently scarred by this trauma.

In our own lives we may draw this moral: *Having rights is not the same as being right.* There's a great tendency to get lost in one's own ego when pursuing one's rights. This is what is meant by the term, "self-righteousness."

- Do you ever, when you have the right of way, yield and let the other driver proceed? Do you identify this as kindness?

- Consider an argument you may be having with your spouse, your parent, your brother or sister. What would be the cost to you to abandon the fight and decide not to contest it any more? Would that turn out to be a kindness, too?

- How important is it in your life that you be "right"? How much has being right cost you so far?

November 16

· ·

> Stop complaining about
> the management of the universe.
> Look around for a place to sow a
> few seeds of happiness.
>
> —Henry Van Dyke

The two Little League teams began their game. A call by the umpire was hotly contested by one team's coach. The other coach jumped into the fray, screaming angrily. The parents on the sidelines contributed catcalls and hoots. Soon, both teams were shouting hotly at each other and at the umpire. The shouting went on. When the umpire restored a semblance of order, 15 minutes had gone by. The game proceeded. The anger from that incident caused everyone to be on edge, ready for the slightest offense to trigger yet another confrontation and, sure enough, another came. A batter's foul ball hit an opposing player on the nose. An ambulance came, its siren almost drowned out by human shouts of defiance and accusation. The umpire canceled the rest of the game because of poor sportsmanship on both sides.

Using all of one's time and energy in the vain pursuit of one's rights, and of a total and perfect fairness, can prevent the accomplishments of *anything* significant. In order to become productively engaged in life, it is often necessary to take what life offers, as it is offered, to decide to make the best of things, and use one's power and creativity to its best advantage.

- Enjoy the moment. Enjoy each experience today without referring to some expectation or inner plan about what the day *ought* to have been. Stop yourself from imposing your need for control on the universe. How does that feel?

- One of our very best friends, Frank Siccone, says, "Surrender to the inevitable success." Can you surrender, just a little bit, to life's flow of experience and reduce your attempts to impose order on it?

- If you used your energy in this way, would it leave you more time and strength to create more kindness in your life and in the world?

November 17

....

"Times are altered with me now,
Nurse Tremlett," replied Mary. "I have
left off living for myself, and I feel my
temper improving already by it."

—Frances Milton Trollop

November 18

....

*T*hey serve God well who
serve his creatures.

—Caroline Sheridan Norton

November 19

....

To live and let live, without clamor
for distinction of recognition; to wait on
divine Love; to write truth first on the
tablet of one's own heart—this is the
sanity and perfection of living
and my human ideal.

—Mary Baker Eddy

November 20

....

In striving for the best, in losing oneself in others, one is lifted above the common material furniture of life, above the gaudy trappings and encumbering paraphernalia, above its contentions and toils, its antagonisms and weariness into a realm of peace which passeth understanding.

—Olympia Brown

November 21

....

Treasure the love you receive above all.
It will survive long after your gold and
good health have vanished.

—Og Mandino

November 22

....

G*uard within yourself that
treasure, kindness. Know how to give
without hesitation, how to lose
without regret, how to acquire
without meanness.*

—George Sand

I'm less than thrilled when I hear the saying, "Nice guys finish last." My heroes have been those who play hard but fair, who compete with a sense of integrity, who pull out that reserve of humor in the face of adversity. Those are the heroes on whom we want to model.

- Who are your personal heroes/heroines?
- What characteristics do they possess that invite your admiration?
- What are your characteristics of kindness?
- Who models after you and why?

November 23

••

> *What do we live for, if it is not*
> *to make life less difficult*
> *for each other.*
>
> —George Eliot

There are people in our lives with whom we have what we refer to as a "laughing relationship." We know that when we're in their company there will be an element of fun. The anticipation is great before each connection. We think about the creativity and playfulness we can bring when meeting them again.

- With whom do you have a laughing relationship?
- What energy do you put into this connection?
- Is it time to reconnect with this person? Could you both benefit from reconnecting?

November 24

B_{ut} when you remember the
suffering, which you have not deserved,
do not think of vengeance, as the small
man does. Remember rather, as the great
remember, that which they have unjustly
suffered, and determine only that such
suffering shall not be possible again
for any human being anywhere.

—Pearl S. Buck

November 25

··

> *It is one of the beautiful compensations of this life that no one can sincerely try to help another without helping himself.*
>
> —Charles Dudley Warner

November 26

....

*The world is in desperate need
of human beings whose own level of
growth is sufficient to enable them to learn
to live and work with others cooperatively
and lovingly, to care for others—not for
what those others can do for you or for
what they think of you, but rather in terms
of what you can do for them.*

—Elisabeth Kubler-Ross

November 27

. . . .

> For humanity has moved forward
> to an era when wrong and slavery are
> being displaced, and reason and justice are
> being recognized as the rule of life.
>
> —Mary Livermore

November 28

....

*The most practical thing
in the world is common sense and
common humanity.*

—Nancy Astor

November 29

....

> Spiritual energy brings compassion into the world. With compassion, we see benevolently our own human condition and the condition of our fellow beings. We drop prejudice. We withhold judgment.
>
> —Christina Baldwin

The approaching turn of the millennium has brought an increased awareness of spirituality. Who are we? Why are we here? We see that we are inextricably linked with one another, with the environment, with all living things. We see that together with the positive energy of many, all good things are possible. Barriers to social progress melt away.

- Do you believe in a Higher Power? If so, what role has it played in your life?
- What do you believe to be your purpose in life?
- How do you view your place as a citizen of the world?

November 30

....

*It doesn't matter who or where you are,
how successful you become in a worldly
way—in a corporate boardroom, in a
hospital operating theater, setting public
policy or managing your private life—
you must care for other people.*

—Barbara Bush

Our society defines success by our material possessions or our career achievements. However
comfortable our material acquisitions make us, in the
final analysis, our worth as human beings is measured
by our compassion for others. Indeed we cannot truly
"make it" in this world alone. The concern we show
others is returned to us ten-fold when we are in need.

- What does success mean to you?
- How can others help you achieve success?
- If you had to choose between winning the lottery
  and living alone, which would you want? Write
  about your choice.

December

December 1

....

*Those who make compassion
an essential part of their lives find the joy
of life. Kindness deepens the spirit and
produces rewards that cannot be
completely explained in words. It is an
experience more powerful than words.
To become acquainted with kindness one
must be prepared to learn new things
and feel new feelings. Kindness is
more than a philosophy of the mind.
It is a philosophy of the spirit.*

—Robert J. Furey

Kindness is the practical expression of one's spirituality. Belief in God or a higher power ought to have some outward manifestation. One's beliefs have to affect one's behavior and attitudes, feelings and the words we choose to say to others. Any belief that does not affect behavior is probably not very strongly held.

- Do you have a sense of your own spirituality, a commitment to some belief system or a religious practice? How deeply held is your commitment to this belief?

- In what ways is your belief expressed in your daily life?

- How do you act out your spirituality toward those closest to you, and toward mankind?

December 2

....

*The cheapest gift I have to give is
kindness, and it is the best.*

—Senator Bob Kerrey

Each year, as the holiday season approaches, one cannot avoid seeing people being encouraged to put themselves in great debt in order to buy presents. One estimate we read was that the average family takes until May of each year to pay off this debt. We see families competing to see who gives the biggest, most expensive gifts. And those who cannot afford these luxuries learn to doubt themselves, feel depressed and unworthy.

We remember not the presents and the wrappings, but the precious time spent with those we love and cherish and enjoy. That *time* is the one gift that stores cannot sell and which can never be replaced. That friend or family member who is irreplaceable in your life—when did you last spend time with them? Just time. The gift of your *presence*, not your presents, is the greatest gift because it implies how very much you value that person, since time is not replaceable and cannot be purchased. Someday, when they or you are gone, the memory of that time spent together will be polished and treasured, and will give great pleasure and solace in your or the person's absence.

- There is someone in your life whose company is precious to you. Can you plan to spend time with your special someone this week?
- Friendships seem to fade when people move away or become involved in some new task or project.

When we get together with such old friends, we sometimes spend the evening simply reminiscing, focusing on the past. That's a danger signal, because relationships need new shared experiences to feed them and keep them growing healthily. Plan something special with an old friend. Spend the time—it's an investment.

December 3

....

You can't give people pride,
but you can provide the kind of
understanding that makes people look
to their inner strengths and find
their own sense of pride.

—Charleszetta Waddles

_____

_____

_____

_____

_____

_____

_____

_____

_____

_____

_____

_____

_____

_____

December 4

....

*If I had known what trouble
you were bearing; what griefs were in
the silence of your face; I would have been
more gentle, and more caring, and tried
to give you gladness for a space.*

—Mary Carolyn Davies

December 5

....

*B*uild a little fence of trust around today;
fill in the space with loving work
and therein stay.

—Mary Frances Butt

_____

_____

_____

_____

_____

_____

_____

_____

_____

_____

_____

_____

_____

_____

_____

December 6

....

> *L*ove understands love;
> it needs no talk.
>
> —Frances Ridley Havergal

_____

_____

_____

_____

_____

_____

_____

_____

_____

_____

_____

_____

_____

_____

_____

_____

_____

December 7

....

*People need joy and kindness
as much as clothing. Some of them
need it far more.*

—Rev. Billy Graham

_____

_____

_____

_____

_____

_____

_____

_____

_____

_____

_____

_____

_____

_____

_____

_____

_____

December 8

"What is real Good?"
I asked in musing mood. Order, said
the law court; Knowledge, said the school;
Truth, said the wise man; Pleasure,
said the fool; Love, said a maiden;
Beauty, said the page; Freedom, said
the dreamer; Home, said the sage;
Fame, said the soldier; Equity, said the seer;
Spake my heart full sadly, "The answer is
not here." Then within my bosom
Softly this I heard: "Each heart holds the
secret; Kindness is the word."

—John Boyle O'Reilly

The single act of kindness to another person can send us into a rising balloon of emotions, and it is not soon forgotten. Knowing this from our own experience, we can still be distracted by many notions of what appropriate goals for ourselves may be. In our striving to achieve, accomplish, gather and earn, we can lose sight of the simplest truths we learned at our parents' knees so long ago. The T-shirt slogan, "Whoever has the most toys when he dies, wins" is revealing of this pointless striving.

We aren't arguing in favor of poverty or the ascetic life. Yet we do point out that the act of attaining just one more *thing* doesn't ever seem to bring into our hearts the satisfaction and sense of peace as that an act of kindness brings.

- What meaning does "real good" have for you?
- To what do you aspire?

December 9

....

We should render a service to a
friend to bind him closer to us, and to an
enemy to make a friend of him.

—Cleobulus

I have had rare moments in my life when I have happened upon someone uniquely talented, controversial, yet inspiring. At first, startled by their ideas, it took courage for me to listen to that voice inside that said, "Don't dismiss this person for their unusual ideas or behaviors, instead look past the obvious to the spirit inside of them." I'm thankful that I did just that and in so doing I was enriched by life's experiences in ways that I never would have been without the gifts of these special people. Sometimes it is necessary to put on "kaleidoscope glasses" to see such a person, to make a conscious decision to look at them from a special perspective.

- Is there someone controversial in your life that you, too, may be uncomfortable around?

- What is that discomfort saying to you?

- If you could see them through kaleidoscope glasses long enough to befriend them or hear their story, what steps would you take?

- If you could step into their shoes, what might they be trying to communicate by their behavior?

December 10

....

Giving presents is a talent;
to know what a person wants, to know
when and how to get it, to give
it lovingly and well.

—Pamela Glenconner

December 11

....

*H*umanity is just a work in progress.

—Tennessee Williams

December 12
....

I have always depended on the
kindness of strangers.

—Tennessee Williams,
A Streetcar Named Desire

December 13

Kindness is the oil that takes the friction out of life.

—Shayna Liora Hinds

_____

_____

_____

_____

_____

_____

_____

_____

_____

_____

_____

_____

_____

_____

_____

_____

_____

_____

December 14

....

It is doubtful whether there is any greater power in human affairs than exerted through the example of love for others.

—Norman Cousins

_____

_____

_____

_____

_____

_____

_____

_____

_____

_____

_____

_____

_____

_____

_____

December 15

....

*T*hree-fourths of the people
you will meet tomorrow are hungering and
thirsting for sympathy. Give it to them,
and they will love you.

—Dale Carnegie

*T*here is more hunger in the world for
love and affection than for bread.

—Anonymous

Hunger is a world disaster: Physical hunger seems omnipresent and contrasts vividly and incomprehensibly with the great surpluses that some people have. We often wonder how this disparity can be allowed to exist. Emotional hunger is also a world disaster: Everywhere we turn there seem to be signs of people in dire need of love, caring and tenderness. And all it may take is a handshake, a hug, a caring touch or a tender word. How can we allow that hunger to exist too?

- Is there someone in your life with whom you could start this positive cycle? Someone you could connect with, to laugh or cry with if necessary?

- Choose one of the following as today's kindness experiment:

  — Call a long-time friend that you haven't connected with in a while.

  — Send a one-minute love call to a family member.

  — Relate a funny story to a colleague.

- Record your experience.

December 16
....

All ordinary violence produces
its own limitations, for it calls forth an
answering violence which, sooner or later,
becomes its equal or its superior. But
kindness works simply and perseveringly;
it produces no strained relations
which prejudice its working; strained
relations which already exist, it relaxes.
Mistrust and misunderstanding,
it puts to flight, and it strengthens itself
by calling forth answering kindness.
Hence it is the furthest reaching and the
most effective of all forces.

All the kindness which a man puts
out into the world works on the heart and
thoughts of mankind, but we are so
foolishly indifferent that we are never in
earnest in the matter of kindness.
We want to topple a great load over,
and yet will not avail ourselves of a lever
which would multiply our
power a hundredfold.

—Albert Schweitzer

Following the recent natural disasters that have
plagued our great country, the media have focused
on the kindnesses that have united neighbor with
neighbor and torn down the barriers of ethnicity and
race. Story after story seeks to prove that these

tragedies are not in vain, that nature's whim cannot crush humanity. Some people feel a sense of camaraderie they might never know otherwise. Like war veterans, disaster survivors find the most awful event of their lives also paradoxically to be the most intense and memorable. Many accidental heroes whose lives have been changed by disaster will seize the moment to change the lives of others. Many of them say, "I was in the right place at the right time," or "Anyone would have done the same thing, given the opportunity."

- What were your feelings as you viewed the nation's natural disasters?

- What did you do—or want to do? Remember that no act of kindness is wasted and even learning about what happened can be of benefit the next time around.

December 17

....

In charity there is no excess.

—Francis Bacon

December 18

....

It's great to be great but it's greater to be human.

—Will Rogers

December 19

· ·

Life is mostly froth and bubble,
Two things stand like stone,
Kindness in another's trouble,
Courage in your own.

—Adam Lindsay Gordon

December 20

··

How kind the visit that ye pay,
like strangers on a rainy day.

—Christopher Smart

December 21

• •

With malice toward none,
with charity for all, with firmness in the
right, as God gives us to see the right,
let us strive on to finish the work we are
in: to bind up the nation's wounds, to care
for him who shall have borne the battle,
and for his widow and his orphan, to do all
which may achieve and cherish a just
and lasting peace among ourselves,
and with all nations.

—Abraham Lincoln,
second inaugural address

December 22

· ·

How beautiful a day can be when
kindness touches it!

—Elliston

Mr. Silva is a well-known gentlemen in our community. His friends are many, but his biggest fan club consists of the children he comes in contact with. You see, he's a retired farmer and still lives on his homestead. Every day, in good weather, he takes his pony and cart to town. He waves and smiles at everyone. If he sees a child he offers the child the opportunity to pet his horse or the dog who rides along with him. If the parents are agreeable, he will take the child for a short ride in the cart.

One day, Mr. Silva passed our house while my young daughter and I were getting the mail. He pulled over and said to me, "Would your baby like to take a peek at my babies?" He proceeded to open a picnic basket with five little kittens inside and held one up for my daughter to cuddle. To this day as he passes she says, "There goes my friend." She can recall the whole event as if it were yesterday.

- What tender childhood events of kindness can you recall?

- What adjectives would you use to describe the actions of those involved?

December 23

....

> *Thou must live for thy neighbor if
> thou wouldst live for thyself.*
>
> —Seneca

Living in a small rural community, we have many opportunities to experience kindness on a regular basis. Our neighbor, for instance, will mow the front of our property when he mows his own. Our postal carrier delivers our mail with a warm greeting. I'm always grateful for these deeds. It is this human connection that encourages me to seek certain community merchants. I seek out those merchants who remember my name, provide me with quality merchandise, tell me about specials or discounts, and will gladly help me out to the car with a heavy load. I've known them to deliver goods to us in an emergency and refuse to take a penny for gas or their time. In return, they have us as customers for life and we even pass on their good graces.

- Who are you a good customer of and why?
- What do they do that keeps you feeling valued time after time?
- How can you replicate this same feeling of being valued for the customers in your workplace?

December 24

....

*Teach us, good Lord, to serve
Thee as Thou deservest:
To give and not to count the cost;
To fight and not to heed the wounds;
To toil and not to seek for rest;
To labour and not to ask for any reward
Save that of knowing that we do Thy will.*

—St. Ignatius Loyola, *Prayer for Generosity*

December 25

···

> *Look at each person you meet*
> *as a person in progress. Then look in*
> *the mirror and see another*
> *person in progress.*
>
> —Carl Rogers

Deliberate Acts of Kindness for Christmas and Hanukkah

Give the gift of kindness for the holidays!

- Holidays can be times of great stress—all the shopping, cooking, visiting, spending, etc.—so take the time to remind yourself what it's all about and calm down, slow down, decide you don't have to spend so very much. Spend more time with family instead of spending more money. The memories of time spent together will be more valuable than some long-forgotten gift.

- When the stress is high, don't hurl insults and criticisms. If you have to disagree, do so with respect, with good listening, with concern for the long-term relationship you have with this person.

- Use the holidays to mend a broken or tattered relationship with a friend or relative. Let go of "who called last" and just call or write today. There'll never be a better time.

- Take a holiday goodie basket to a sick or unhappy friend or neighbor. Send flowers to a shut-in.

- Go out of your way to be extra kind to store personnel. They are terribly overworked and strained at this time of year. Many are temporary workers, very aware that they will be terminated at the end of the holidays and will get no benefits. They may be trying to earn a little extra to treat their loved ones.

- Make a *kinder schedule* for yourself at this time. If certain things aren't urgent, postpone them. Don't say "yes" to more than you can reasonably accomplish.

- Frame old photos that special people might appreciate.

- Let go of something you have no control over. People do not base their love for you on how much you give them.

- Talk with your family about their favorite holiday traditions and try to include something special for each one in your holiday plans. Ask them to help you make those plans come true. Don't do it all alone!

- Prepare a second holiday meal along with yours. It's not as difficult as doing a separate meal. Deliver the meal to a shut-in.

- Spread peanut butter on a pine cone, roll it in birdseed and hang it on a tree outside your home, to be kind to winter birds.

- Send a holiday basket to a friend at college. Fill it with cards, stamps, music, decorations for their room, etc.

- Contact a local foster care agency or adult care facility and send cards to those who have few family members or close connections and rarely get mail.

- Do you know someone who's caring for an elderly parent or invalid? Offer them *respite care*, where you take over for a few hours so they can get out, do some shopping, or just rest and recuperate from the stress of constantly caring for someone.

- Whatever you do for yourself, for family or for friends, keep it simple. People would much rather have you, your good spirits and happy smile than a harried, exhausted buyer of extravagant gifts. Collect good memories rather than collecting more things for next year's garage sale.

- Let a harried parent with little kids get into the line in front of you.

- Build a nice fire and offer a warm beverage to sip in front of the fireplace to someone you love.

- Hug your family a little more this year. They need the "skin nourishment."

- Give blood—it's always needed.

- Forgive any rude or thoughtless people you meet today. They may be too wounded to be kind or caring right now. Model for them the kind of person you'd like them to become.

- Let other cars in line in front of you and wave thanks to those who do it for you.

- If you know anyone who has lost family members since last holiday season, invite them to be part of your celebration, or at least call them and let them know that they are in your heart.

- Record an uplifting holiday greeting on your answering machine. Include a favorite poem or prayer, and some sweet, meaningful music.

- Keep the spirit of this holiday season uppermost in your mind. While many people are only thinking about what they have to *do*, you can, instead, think about how you have to *be* in order to *get* a happy, safe, caring, loving and nourishing holiday with friends and family.

December 26

. . . .

*The proper use of imagination
is to give beauty to the world . . . the gift
of imagination is used to cast over the
commonplace work-a-day world a veil of
beauty and make it throb with
our esthetic enjoyment.*

—Lin Yutang

December 27

....

Count no day lost in which
you waited your turn, took only your
share and sought advantage
over no one.

—Robert Brault

_____

_____

_____

_____

_____

_____

_____

_____

_____

_____

_____

_____

_____

_____

_____

_____

December 28

· ·

It is easy to make the mistake and think that someone's problems are just like yours and therefore can be solved in just the same way yours were. This can lead to an unconsciously arrogant sort of helping. At the airport baggage claim, there's a sign: "Be careful, many bags look alike." We are all carrying bags and baggage in our lives and some may look alike. But each contains unique things, experiences and history that no one else shares. Listen to those you would help. Become aware of the totality of their uniqueness. When you do, your perception of them will be truly humble. You'll let them into your understanding, and any help you may offer will come from this humility.

—Meladee McCarty

December 29

Kindness may be undeserved.
And what rejoices man's heart is precisely
what he is given as a sheer gift . . .
a gift which he has not deserved.

—Rudolf Bultmann

A teacher friend shared with us that she was shopping in her local food store and discovered some brown paper sacks that would be perfect for her second-graders to use to make mock bee hives. Asked the cost of the 120 sacks needed, the clerk called for a price check. By the time the clerk came back with the cost of the 120 bags, someone waiting in line had donated the entire amount anonymously. I wonder what the children in her class would have thought of this project had they known that there was someone out there enjoying their joy.

- If you weren't allowed to give money, what outrageous anonymous act of kindness could you come up with?

- What are you waiting for?

December 30

....

*T*he world is a classroom;
        the lesson, love.

—Barbara Jordan

Despite our age, we never really leave school. Whether we are eight or 80, the ultimate lesson is the same: love. It matters not how high an IQ we possess. If we do not learn that love is the answer, we will fail the test of life. Look around you—every day there is an opportunity to love.

- How many different kinds of love can you identify?
- What lessons have you learned from love?
- What other lessons can you learn from love?

December 31

Snowflakes are one of nature's most fragile things, but just look what they can do when they stick together!

—Verna M. Kelly

_____
_____
_____
_____
_____
_____
_____
_____
_____
_____
_____
_____
_____
_____
_____
_____
_____

About the Authors

••

Dr. **Hanoch McCarty** has been speaking professionally all around the world for over 28 years. He is the president of Hanoch McCarty & Associates, a seminar and training company that helps corporations, organizations, schools and individuals reach their goals and achieve their fullest potential congruent with their highest integrity.

He is a founding member of the National Council for Self-Esteem, was a professor of education at Cleveland State University in Ohio for nearly 20 years and was a single parent with full custody of two children for 12 years! Hanoch is the coauthor with his wife, Meladee, of *Acts of Kindness: How to Create a Kindness Revolution*, and *A Year of Kindness: 365 Ways to Spread Sunshine,* and with Jack Canfield, Mark Victor Hansen and Meladee McCarty is coauthor of *A 4th Course of Chicken Soup for the Soul*.

Hanoch conducts seminars for managers, executives, small business owners and employee groups, parents, teachers, corporations, associations, and government agencies. He has received many standing ovations for his exciting, unique and thought-provoking style. Audiences come away delighted, informed and empowered. He is famous for completely customizing his presentations to fit the needs and themes of your conference or training program.

He and Meladee have been conducting *Kindness Seminars* for adult groups all over the United States and Canada. These have included workshops on:

- Kindness in Couple Relationships
- Kindness in the Family
- Kindness Strategies for Dramatically Increasing Employee Productivity and Motivation

Hanoch has also been presenting *Kindness Rallies* for school assembly programs:

- Kindness Is a Chain Reaction: Creating a Kinder World Through Your Own Actions
- The Ten Secrets of Life Success

You can receive a brochure describing these programs by sending a stamped, self-addressed #10 envelope to:

Dr. Hanoch McCarty
The Kindness Revolution
P.O. Box 66
Galt, CA 95632

If you are interested in booking a program for your group, call Dr. McCarty at (209) 745-2212 or fax (209) 745-2252.

*M*eladee McCarty is a program specialist in special education for the Sacramento County Office of Education in California.

She has an extensive teaching background and works to find appropriate placements for children who have significant emotional challenges.

Meladee has worked with teachers, counselors and administrators, as well as classified personnel, and has conducted hundreds of workshops, training seminars, and educational events all over the United States as well as in Norway.

Along with her husband, Dr. Hanoch McCarty, she presented the opening keynote address at the seventh Annual National Adolescence Conference in Atlanta, and has presented at many national and regional events including the World Safe For Children Conference in Miami, attended by representatives from 25 nations.

A member of the National Association for Self-Esteem, she has designed and presented a wide variety of training events that emphasize the key role played by self-esteem in student achievement.

She is coauthor, with her husband, of *Acts of Kindness: How to Create a Kindness Revolution* and *A Year of Kindness: 365 Ways to Spread Sunshine*. She is also coauthor, along with Hanoch McCarty, Jack Canfield and Mark Victor Hansen, of *A 4th Course of Chicken Soup for the Soul*.

You can reach her at:

Hanoch McCarty & Associates
P.O. Box 66
Galt, CA 95632
(209) 745-2212 • (209) 745-2252 FAX

A Call for Kindness Stories!

....

We are always writing new articles and books on kindness. There are certainly enough stories in the media about rudeness, violence, selfishness and negativity, aren't there? We want to redress the balance. We are convinced that there are really more acts of kindness in the world (which go unreported) than there are acts of negativity. We want to tell the world about them and you can help us!

Do you know a good kindness story? Have you done an act of kindness that you're proud of? Has someone done a kindness to you? When you tell the world about a kindness you become a "door-opener"—you allow other people to begin to visualize the positive alternatives open to them. More people become able to see themselves as kind or as able to become kind when they read or hear a good kindness story. Tell your story.

If you don't think you're a "good writer," don't worry about it. We will help to rewrite your story if you need that help. The most important thing is to tell us the story.

Do you know a good story about kindness? Have you read one somewhere that we ought to know about? Tell us about it. Send us a copy if you can—especially with information about the source of the story (who wrote it, where it was published, etc.)—so that we can contact the authors or publishers for permission to reproduce it.

If your story gets selected for one of our publications, we'll ask your permission before we use it and we'll give you credit for writing or for submitting it. And you'll have the knowledge that you've helped to create a real *Kindness Revolution* in our world. Sharing kindness stories can be your ministry and your blessing, too.

Send your stories to:

The Kindness Revolution Story Editors
P.O. Box 66
Galt, CA 95632

No stories can be returned. Please keep your own copy of anything submitted. Remember that certain stories may submitted by a number of people simultaneously. In those cases, if we use a story, we'll credit the first person to submit it.